THIS BOOK IS FEMINIST

WRITTEN BY JAMIA WILSON
ILLUSTRATED BY AURÉLIA DURAND

Frances Lincoln
Children's Books

CONTENTS

Growing up, I often heard negative messages and myths in the media about what feminism is and who people who identify as feminists are. Why? Mostly because of feminism being defined in one dimension instead of in the fullness of its immense capacity to hold and support us all.

While the word "feminism" emerged in the English language in the late eighteen hundreds, women and gender nonconforming people's battle against bias, domination, and prejudice has been described in terms of the first, second, third, and fourth "waves" ever since. As with all categories and structures, the lines and terms that define each of these are up for debate but are commonly understood to hold shared values, tensions, and historic markers.

Feminists are diverse and have varying theories of change and approaches to reaching our goals. So, I often refer to the work I do as understanding and honoring various "feminism(s)" to acknowledge that identities, experiences, histories, and resources impact our focus and the vantage point that guides our ideas and actions.

For years, I've been reading stale obituaries about "feminism's looming end" in the media and hearing several elder feminists ask "Where are the young women?" without fully exploring how movement spaces and organizations could be more intergenerational.

Now I'm thrilled that feminists continue to create insurgent ground with their voices, art, and complexities to constantly open up the story of who we are, who we hope to be, and who is included in our quest for equality and justice.

Jamia Wilson

CHAPTER ONE

What does Feminism mean?

"Feminism is a movement to end sexism, sexist exploitation, and oppression." —bell hooks

"Feminists are people that care about immigrants and workers and the environment and labor rights, and of course reproductive rights, LGBTQIA+ rights. These I call feminist values." —Dolores Huerta

"How could you not want to include the persecuted trans women or nonbinary folk so you have more comrades to fight against gendered oppression?" —Janet Mock

"...Of course men can and should be feminists too. It just means that we are getting rid of the gender roles that didn't always exist. Old languages didn't have he and she. They didn't have gender pronouns; people were people." —Gloria Steinem

BEYOND A TREND

Merriam-Webster's Dictionary made history when it chose feminism as its featured "word of the year" in 2017. The dictionary shared that online searches for the word rose 70% that year. So, what happened that year? And why was everyone suddenly googling a term dear to my heart?

This was the year of the **#MeToo**[1] movement, ignited by survivor activist Tarana Burke against sexual harassment and abuse; the aftermath of the record-breaking Women's March, which mobilized five million people globally; and the historic upsurge of women running for elected office in the United States.

That year, I scrolled through news headlines and comment sections on social media about feminism's #trending moment, and thought about how much had changed and, sadly, what has stayed the same since the word was first described as "the qualities of females" in an English dictionary in the 1840s.

I thought about the over **12,000 years of sexism** that led to this moment and the known and mostly unknown people whose work, art, voices, and partnerships pushed back at a structure that benefits and positions one group of people in power over others throughout history.

OUR HISTORY

Historically, as **cisgender** (people who are not trans) men began to rule the majority of societies worldwide, women and girls held less **autonomy**, or ability to make choices for themselves. (These societies are known as patriarchal human social systems, where men whose gender identity matches the one they were assigned at birth hold primary control, power, property, and leadership.)

A widely held understanding is that what began as more egalitarian (equal) hunter and gathering cultures moved toward farming. Control and ownership of the farm began to be passed down the male line. Over time, this model became reinforced within religion, education, and government.

Too often, when stereotypes become rooted as "the norm," false ideas mask themselves as truth. There are so many ways to be a human, but we receive messages at an early age that we're expected to behave or express ourselves in a certain manner, or wear specific colors. (Did you ever witness a young boy being told that "boys don't cry," or an outspoken little girl being told off for being "bossy" and not being "ladylike?")

This became the norm in many cultures around the world, especially as people moved from one country to another, either from migration or colonialism. This is how the false idea spread of a 'natural order of things' being determined by biology. But we know this is not how things always were or should be.

A lot of what is recorded and understood about feminism occurred between the seventeenth century and today. However, the fight against imbalances of power began much earlier: from Andal, an eighth-century Tamil woman poet who boldly rejected gendered "wifely" duties, to fifteenth-century Italian-French author Christine de Pizan's imagining of a women-only utopia. Modern-day conversations about gender equality are rooted in the seeds their lineage planted long, long ago.

There are so many ways to be a human

INTERSECTIONAL FEMINISM

Although I was happy people were looking up the definition of feminism, I yearned for the dictionary to speak more about the feminism I embrace and live for—one that includes and uplifts the connection between:

racial justice, disability, immigration, LGBTQIA+ rights, labor rights, reproductive justice, environmental justice, and feminism.

The feminism that paved the way for me was **intersectional** feminism that emerged from black feminist thinkers, including Kimberlé Crenshaw, bell hooks, Audre Lorde, and the Combahee River Collective.

My own Black feminist ancestors by blood and through spirit taught me to understand feminism through questions about who is left out and who is on the margins.

How can we move the people who know most about the issues their communities are facing

to the center instead of the sidelines?

Reading Indigenous Australian artist, activist, and academic Lilla Watson's words also shaped my perspective. She declared, "If you have come here to help me, you are wasting your time. But if you have come because your liberation is bound up with mine, then let us work together." When I later discovered that Watson felt uncomfortable being credited for a motto that emerged as a part of her aboriginal activist group in Queensland's collective experience in the 1970s, I gained a valuable lesson about the importance and impact of solidarity.

The definition in the dictionary described the fundamental root of the issues without getting to the heart of what feminism is continuously evolving to be: a space for liberation, equality, and justice for all.

CALL TO ACTION

- *Does the modern-day dictionary definition make sense to you? Does it need to expand?*
- *Who do you imagine when you think about feminism and whose lives it enhances?*
- *Do you see yourself?*
- *Who is left out?*

ABILITY

CLASS

APPEARANCE

RACE

AGE

DISABILITY

GENDER
IDENTITY

LANGUAGE

INTERSECTIONALITY

A term coined by Kimberlé Crenshaw to describe the interconnected nature of social categorizations, such as race, class, and gender, as they apply to an individual or group, creating overlapping systems of discrimination.

IMMIGRATION STATUS

SEX

PHYSICAL HEALTH

MENTAL HEALTH

RELIGION

NATIONALITY

FERTILITY

CULTURE

CHAPTER TWO

The name game:

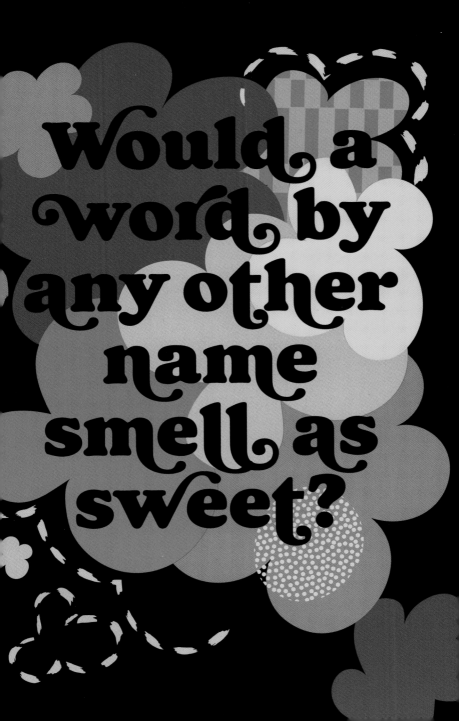

NAME GAMES

If you're still struggling with the concept of taking on a label, I get it. Mark my words, I'd rather collaborate with folks with shared values versus pull hairs over whether their labels "100% align" with mine. The late author and poet Maya Angelou said "I am a feminist. I've been female for a long time now. It'd be stupid not to be on my own side."

Like her, I'm a proud feminist because I know that being on the side of the most marginalized people, which is most often women and nonbinary people, is akin to being on "my own side." In our imperfect world, if conditions are such that those who have the least are taken care of, we will all be closer to freedom and justice.

With that said, I also understand that the term itself carries historic weight because of myths, stereotypes, and media misconceptions about who feminists are and what we think.

Like any group of people, feminists are diverse and might call themselves by many names. For example, I also identify as a **womanist**, as defined by writer Alice Walker to honor the experiences and stories of Black women and to resist anti-Blackness within mainstream white feminist institutions and conversations. Similarly, some of my friends identify as **mujeristas** who are Latinx women and non-binary folks who fight for liberation for themselves and their community.

There's nothing kind, compassionate, or caring about abuse of power or inequality, period.

In our imperfect world, if conditions are such that those who have the least are taken care of, we will all be closer to freedom and justice.

Sound simple? Good. If not, let's dive deeper into why some forms of sexism and misogyny are sugarcoated or brushed off by some as "coming from a good place," "being traditional," or a valid point of disagreement.

Close your eyes and think about who you've been taught is the norm, the default, and the center of power in our communities and in our culture. When I think about the fact that our 46 United States presidents have been mostly white cisgender men with only one person of color, it is clear that barriers to access and outdated attitudes about leadership and power persist.

Although it might feel like a stretch, a stale comment from an old-school family friend at dinner about how "women should be guided and protected by men" or "women have unique strengths to run the household, so it's important that men work outside the home to care for them" can affect elections, media, and policies. They have a direct impact on how people vote on the laws that govern our lives. When tired expressions

about gender identity are casually mentioned, absorbed, and, worse, *accepted* as overarching truths, we are all limited.

While it's fine for people to have varying views, it is never okay to deny anyone's human rights, equality, or dignity in the process. Much of what we hear on TV focuses on more obvious, hostile sexism. But the reality is that the clutches of what is known as "**benevolent sexism**" (which in itself is an **oxymoron**) seeps into the fabric of our schools, institutions, media, political systems, and culture.

You may recognize it in the form of the "damsel in distress" cartoons you watched as a child, or savior stories you read or heard about in the news, about women needing protecting from men to stay safe. The mindset that fosters these ideas often affirms that women are valuable when—and if—they comply with cisgender men being in charge, in control, or in leadership of everyone else.

When tired expressions about gender identity are casually mentioned, absorbed, and, worse, accepted as overarching truths, we are all limited.

If any of this sounds familiar, take a moment to think about how feminism has paved a way to change the conversation. Take an opportunity to thank a feminist every day for the ways in which your own life has been made possible due to others' courage, from wearing trousers (yes, that was a thing!) to fighting for equal pay. For example, I often thank my wall portrait of Ida B. Wells for fighting for Black women's right to vote, even though she was undermined by some white **suffragists** during her time. If you're stumped, look to the luminaries at the opening of each chapter.

Whether or not you choose to carry the banner, **the feminist wins we benefit from, and may even take for granted, came to us because someone was willing to stand up, speak up, and make a change.**

DOES IT "CLICK" FOR YOU?

What did I do to celebrate my awakening or, as many call it, my personal feminist "click" moment? Although I agreed with gender justice early on after hearing my family talk about headlines in the news, I didn't connect feminism with my identity until my teen years.

That's why I've decided to honor the "aha" moment that transformed my life by writing about how watching Professor Anita Hill's testimony[2] before the US Senate Judiciary Committee on TV in 1991 inspired me to speak truth to power. Professor Hill's courage in the face of injustice gave me words for a sense of knowing that all people deserve freedom, justice, and access to their fullest potential. It also connected me to my mother and grandmother's generation. It was a life-defining moment for me.

If you think back long enough, your "click" moment may have been caught up in the everyday nature of how we learn to value some people's power, position, ideas, and values over others, and over ourselves.

My beliefs later guided me to move thousands of miles from home to attend a boarding school started by eighteenth-century **Bluestocking feminists**, and later to devote much of my activism and career to the cause. But unlike my sweet sixteen, or my graduation speech during my senior year, no cake or other fanfare honored the time I committed myself to the purpose of equality for all people—including myself. And why not?

In the years that have passed, I've realized that my recognition of the idea that freedom cannot exist for some when anyone is left behind or undermined informs every part of my life.

CALL TO ACTION

- *What's your "click" moment? Has any idea, movement, community, or mindset moved your heart and mind?*
- *How will you celebrate it?*
- *What will the next generation thank YOU for?*

CHAPTER THREE

Not Your Mama's Feminism

COME AS WE ARE

As I mentioned earlier, Anita Hill's testimony changed my life and brought me closer to older women—including my mother and my grandmother. Their experiences with sexual harassment helped shape my views. I looked to them for examples of how to think about policies, ideas, and changemaking. But when I was twelve, I discovered how my generation had its own differences and causes.

It came to me in a surprising package, via MTV. Nirvana, a '90s grunge band from Washington unpredictably transformed the music industry with their hit "Come as You Are." Famed for breaking through top music charts with rebellious lyrics and a forceful sound, Nirvana's bitingly refreshing roar made millions of people aware of social issues, including gender identity, feminism, sexual assault, and other abuses of power through their music videos, performances, and interviews.

At the time, I was living as a young expat in Saudi Arabia where media censorship blocked access to what was deemed "controversial content" from home. Nirvana's melodic embrace of gender fluidity, nod to LGBTQIA+ rights, and odes to self-expression slipped under the radar. Their grunge anthem "Smells Like Teen Spirit" gave young people permission to celebrate being themselves, own their voices, and speak up to authority.

This was my first understanding that the feminism I associated with my mother's generation looked and felt different than my own.

I understood from my mother's Black feminist textbooks about the suffrage movement and the women's liberation movements of the '60s and '70s in the United States and Europe that women of color had different experiences, perspectives, and considerations about how to define gender justice work, tactics, history, and activism. So, I was puzzled that listening to a band helmed by three white cis men who lived thousands of miles away from me began to expand my thinking about gender justice.

I wondered if it had to do with **internal conditioning** to look for leadership from people with the most power and privilege in our culture. When I learned that graffiti scrawled by Kurt Cobain's close friend Kathleen Hanna, the lead singer of the **"Riot Girl"** punk band Bikini Kill, onto his bedroom wall inspired his hit music, I dug deeper to learn about his motivations for writing about feeling like an outsider in a culture that too often punishes those who fail to conform to its limitations.

As I listened to an interview where Cobain confessed that he felt alienated by what would now be described as "**toxic masculinity**" in high school, I began thinking about the meaning of allyship without having a label for it yet.

"Because I couldn't find any male friends that I felt compatible with, I hung out with girls a lot. I just always felt that women weren't treated with respect," he said. After saying that "women are totally oppressed" and condemning the use of **misogynistic** words, Cobain went on to talk about awakening to the fact that some of his formerly favorite bands wrote about sexist topics and represented women in ways that treated them like objects instead of people.

PUNK ROCK FEMINISM RULES

BIKINI KILL

In addition to sharing about his exploration of his own sexual identity, he credited the anger he felt due to his mother's **homophobia** in response to him showing affection toward a male friend, and the pain he experienced as a result of his disability. Something about the dots Cobain connected when he spoke about his own suffering, felt like empathy, and in some ways, **solidarity** to me.

Although Cobain could never walk in my shoes due to his privilege and power as a wealthy, white, cisgender man in the global limelight, I viewed him as a bridge to a new path. Thanks to our mutual love for Nirvana, I was able to engage some of my previously dismissive classmates in conversations about the issues I cared about related to street harassment, sexist name-calling, racism, and homophobia. Many of their lyrics and messages created channels to normalize dialogues that were laced with stigma before this band made them cool, accessible, and safer to discuss at school. Strange as it may seem, a grunge band that looked nothing like me, and their righteous cultural critique were a call to arms. Their music brought topics to life I yearned to talk more about and explore emotionally and politically.

When my mom told me to stop listening to Nirvana during family dinner, I told her that I was riveted by music that challenged norms and openly celebrated the complexities of identity in public. Always keen to discuss society and culture, she asked me what

> **"I think this music is teaching me that when we truly learn to 'come as we are,' we become who we are."**

I learned that was so important that it couldn't wait until after we digested our barbecued chicken and yams.

"Mom," I said, "I think this music is teaching me that when we truly learn to 'come as we are,' we become who we are." As she gazed upon me with a deep stare, I began to reinsert the headphones, proud that my point was clearly taken.

Without missing a beat, my Mom handed me my soiled plate with a chuckle. "Well, baby, it's great that this Nirvana has you excited about being who you are and a feminist, and now you need to 'come as you are' to this kitchen as soon as we're done and do dishes, because Mama has been working all day at my job and now, here in this house. Come to think of it, get your Dad over here to help too."

There and then, I understood that perhaps my "click" moments might not be my Mama's feminism. Although the root issues are the same—it was okay for me to be open to exploring meaning in new ways that made sense to my context and community. And I hope you will explore your own feminism too, and find your own click moments.

I evolved my own thinking, based on the experiences of my life that outraged me into action. I also learned that listening to my Mom's experiences with curiosity instead of judgment might help me do the same when my future child came in singing new notes to our ever-emerging songs of freedom and justice.

CALL TO ACTION

Take a moment to jot down some thoughts about your own relationship to feminism, and your family.

1. Has pop culture ever taught you anything unexpectedly about the way you see the world?
2. How does your definition of equality, justice, and feminism line up with the people who raised you? How does it differ?
3. What would you like to share with the next generation?
4. What do you wish you could talk about with older generations but don't feel comfortable sharing?
5. What is one thing you can do this week to engage an elder in your life in conversation about the issues you care about?

CHAPTER FOUR

Identity

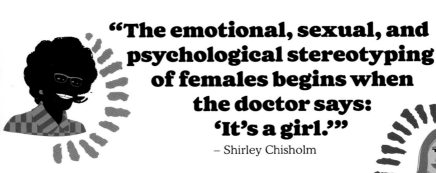

> # "The emotional, sexual, and psychological stereotyping of females begins when the doctor says: 'It's a girl.'"
> – Shirley Chisholm

> # "Identity politics is ... what we used to call civil rights."
> – Samantha Bee, *Full Frontal*

ARE YOU A BLANK SLATE?

"Are we born a blank slate?" my teacher inquired as she passed out pieces of stark-white paper to illustrate her question. As we discussed philosopher John Locke's essay from 1689 comparing the mind to a piece of "white paper, void of all characters," my thoughts wandered to the present.

While half-listening to her lecture, I contemplated whether or not I entered the world as a "tabula rasa" (a blank slate)— and if in fact I had, somehow, participated in forming my sense of identity.

I thought of one of my earliest photos, taken a week after my birth in our apartment in South Carolina. Adorned in a lacy pastel headband covering sparse dark curls and twinkling gold stud earrings, I was the picture of what American media and society defined as Black girlhood.

Although the 1980s-era TV, magazine, and product advertisements that set standards about how children should look mainly focused on golden-haired white children, my appearance matched rigid stereotypes about gender.

Fast-forward to the present, and I now have friends raising a new generation of children to see how their own gender identity and expression emerges, instead of actively giving them the gender roles: 'girl' or 'boy.' Looking back, my clothing and hairstyles reflected and reinforced the gender norms of my time.

After the blank slate discussion, I asked my parents why they chose to pierce my ears only days after my birth.

Although I loved the "grown-up" feeling of having pierced ears when some of my classmates were forced to wait until their thirteenth birthday, something bothered me about not having a role in deciding why and when sharp little spikes were pushed into my sensitive skin. What if I wanted to express myself a different way? How did they know I wanted to wear earrings and a pink headband? My father furrowed his brow and responded, "You didn't have that much hair, so we got you earrings and a headband so people would know you were a girl."

Almost in unison, my mother echoed his point, "You were our little doll baby, but you needed more hair." She tittered, "I didn't want people asking if you were a boy or a girl, so until it was evident, we made sure it was clear." Every few years, I'd bring up the conversation again to perplexed stares and queries about why having my ears pierced before I could consent still bugged me.

It all came to a head when my grandmother, who by the way never had pierced ears in over ninety years of life, said, "After all, you're such a 'girly-girl' anyway, and you love to wear earrings, so it worked out. I'd get

> **"You didn't have that much hair, so we got you earrings and a headband so people would know you were a girl."**

it if you were a tomboy like your aunt." Finally, it made sense to me how even in a family full of self-described feminists, and folks who blazed trails by doing things that some people believed they weren't worthy of doing because of their skin color, economic class, and/or gender, **we still held tightly to gender roles and stereotypes with a firm clenched fist.**

When I reflect upon those photos today, I don't see a blank slate. Instead, I see a bright, joyful, and curious child who was surrounded by love. But at the same time, I notice new things about my much younger baby self, the middle-class, visually-disabled, African American child staring back at me telling me who she is. It's impossible now to separate how the identities she was born with and those society imposed upon her shaped her life and her relationship to power in our society.

To be clear, my presentation and experience of my gender identity has afforded me unearned privilege because I largely conform to gender norms within dominant culture and society in the United States. While my situation clearly pales in comparison to people who have grown up in homes and communities where they face abuse, isolation, and/or ridicule because of their gender identity, I learned a lot from exploring my personal discomfort with gender stereotyping and rituals within my own family.

I remembered other, sometimes painful 'aha-moments' that taught me to ask questions and explore gender identity, and how it links with all of our intersecting identities. After pinpointing the initial moment where I learned that my compliance with my family's understanding of how little Black girls of my economic class should look, behave, and navigate the world, a zoetrope of experiences came to mind.

Like when I once overheard an older relative voice her concern to my mother that sending me to an all-girls school would "turn me queer," and to my delight, my mother responded, "And so, what if she was?" To the moment where my diverse group of friends and I were chased out of a shopping center by a group of racist skinheads who screamed at us for holding hands and "promoting Lesbianism" and "race mixing," and to moments I'm deeply ashamed of when I perpetuated the problem, like when a friend admitted she had a crush on me and I freaked out, got angry with her for making me uncomfortable, and ran away. Our relationship was never the same, and the ugliness was mine to own. The culture of fear I absorbed poured toxicity out onto someone else, pushing them further into hiding themselves because of my fear about being seen as an outsider. And the list goes on, and on. Instead, I could have said to my friend: "I'm really glad you told me. Do you want to talk more?"

BUT, I'M AN INDIVIDUAL, #AMIRITE?

The construction of identity in our society has everything to do with power structures, and less to do with being an "individual" (as we're so often taught in **"western"** culture).

Once I opened my eyes to the smallest moments where seeds were planted about my own sense of identity, it made me aware of the larger instances in my life where this has been the case.

So much of early written perspectives on feminism in the United States and Europe were rooted in individualist perspectives authored by highly educated, affluent, white cisgender women, usually in heterosexual relationships and traditional family structures.[3]

In contrast, the oft-misunderstood phrase "identity politics" was coined by Black feminist Barbara Smith and the Combahee River Collective in 1974.[4]

The Combahee River Collective defined their politics by expressing outright that they were acknowledging their points of "ideological opposition" with white feminism while also being linked in collaboration with Black men in the fight against racism. Simultaneously, they acknowledged being in the midst of a struggle with Black men due to sexism, patriarchy, and heterosexism. They proclaimed, 'The most profound and potentially most radical politics come directly out of our own identity.'

When I finally encountered the Combahee River Collective manifesto in high school and began to explore queer and gender theory by Riki Wilchins, I came to understand that gender identity is much more complex than the limited binaries we've been taught to conform to, believe in, and protect.

Our gender is determined by our experience of it, beyond what our community may expect or pressure us to fit into. Our gender can be fluid instead of fixed. We can show and experience our gender through the pronouns we use (mine are she/her) the labels we decide to reject or embrace, how we choose to dress and act, and how those expressions make us feel in our minds, bodies, and spirits. Humans can identify with multiple genders or no genders, and/or move between them.

While it remains woefully true that social expectations about gender identity can impact our social, cultural, work, and legal rights, whether or not we fit stereotypes about how we should present or behave should not determine our freedom or access to live our lives with dignity and justice. Moreover, until we exist in a world where transgender and **gender nonconforming people** can live and thrive, none of us are truly free.

As an LGBTQIA+ ally who still has lots to learn and unlearn about how not to impose my own fears, expectations, and internalized oppression about how to express gender, I'm committed to doing the work needed so that I don't continue to pass on traditions of unconscious and conscious harm and shame that hold us all back from liberation.

Feminism and transgender rights are intrinsically linked. Both are fighting against the gender binary, patriarchy, and gender expectations. We can't ignore this connection and must make sure our feminism is inclusive.

> **Our gender is determined by our experience of it, beyond what our community may expect or pressure us to fit into.**

PROUD

CALL TO ACTION

Write down the following prompt and take a moment to recall some of your earliest memories. Fill in the blanks below with gender, race, class, religion, culture, or another form of identity. Jot down a few sentences about each query:

- I remember the first time I became aware of my _____identity.
-I remember the first time I felt othered because of my _____identity.
-I remember the first time I learned about my _____identity and its relationship to power or lack of power in our society and or culture.

Ask yourself whether you recall ever dismissing, harming, or undermining someone because they didn't fit into your idea of how they should experience or express their identity. Reflect on what you learned from that and write a letter to yourself about what you pledge to do differently and how to be more accountable next time.

EQUALITY

Equality means giving everyone **the same opportunities**, treatment, and support. Use this box as an example of equality. All three people are given the same box to view the scenery—but can all three people see the same thing? Who is left out? Who sees the most? Who is shortchanged?

EQUITY

Equity is about giving people **what they need** in order to make things fair and equal. Based on circumstances, it gives more to those who need it, and less to those who don't, so they can reach their potential. By giving different sized and shaped boxes, everyone can see the view. *Equity is how we get equal.*

"I ask no favor for my sex; all I ask of our brethren is that they take their feet off our necks." —US Supreme Court Justice Ruth Bader Ginsburg

"No struggle can ever succeed without women participating side by side with men. There are two powers in the world; one is the sword and the other is the pen. There is a third power stronger than both, that of women." —Malala Yousafzai, Nobel Prize Laureate

"Women of all colors have always been on these battle lines, and it is my own feminist mother, daughter and grandchildren that I have in mind when I do this work for equality." —Carol Jenkins, CEO and co-President, Equal Rights Amendment Coalition

"Courage is a decision you make to act in a way that works through your own fear for the greater good as opposed to pure self-interest. Courage means putting at risk your immediate self-interest for what you believe is right."
—Derrick Bell, lawyer, professor, civil rights activist

CHAPTER FIVE

Justice

"Freedom is like taking a bath: You got to keep doing it every day."
—Florynce Kennedy, attorney and feminist activist

"We are going to be the kids you read about in textbooks." —Emma Gonzalez, gun control activist, Parkland shooting survivor

"TRUST YOUR OWN OUTRAGE"

I grew up in a southern family with deep roots in the American Civil Rights Movement. Early on, they taught me that we valued justice and freedom for all people. Throughout my childhood, I heard stories my parents and grandparents told me about their participation in sit-ins, marches, voter registration campaigns, and other actions to confront the policies and practices that impacted their lives in the racially segregated South. From Mom specifically, I learned that Black women's bodies were often treated like battlefields for those in opposition to equality.

Among many other accounts of injustice, from having her dog stolen by the Ku Klux Klan hate group to being arrested and sprayed by water hoses after marching against racist **Jim Crow laws**, my mom recalled the trauma of surviving 1968's Orangeburg massacre in her South Carolina college community.

I still get chills when I remember the nightmares my mother had on the days after she recounted the mass shooting when police opened fire on a crowd of two hundred unarmed students protesting segregation, killing three and injuring twenty-eight people—one of whom was a pregnant woman who miscarried as a result of the brutality. My mother explained that while all demonstrators were in danger of being attacked, women were often specifically targeted. Shuddering, she explained that the vigilantes and officers who brutally battered her and her female companions often intensified their assaults to threaten Black women's dignity, and to incite the patriarchal anger of male protesters.

Years later, I thought of her experience in the midst of Black Lives Matter uprisings following the tragic deaths of George Floyd, Breonna Taylor, Rayshard Brooks, Riah Milton, Dominique Fells, and so many others due to state-supported racial violence.

Through her firsthand accounts and from my own studies that followed, I began to understand how racial and sexual harassment and abuse were and still are used as tools to bolster the charade of cis white male superiority and to conjure fear.

While I was learning about this period in my family history from my mom's side of the family, my father and grandmother taught me about the plight of my cousin, Joan Little.

Not long after my mother survived the massacre, which was the first mass shooting of its kind to happen on a US university campus prior to the Kent State and Jackson State murders of student protesters, Joan was arrested and locked up for defending herself by using deadly force to stop a white jailer who attempted to rape her in prison.

Only a few decades prior to Joan's trial, in the 1940s, it had been almost unheard of for Black victims of sexual violence to receive justice in the courts. Over the course of the 1940s, '50s and '60s, thousands of Black people and allies mobilized to defend women's human rights, bodily integrity, and dignity, including activist Rosa Parks. But throughout 1974 and '75, women of color, organizers, and grassroots advocates rallied together for my cousin's cause. Both Black-led and some mostly white feminist groups called for her freedom in the name of sexual assault victims' rights.

Recognizing the power of the grassroots movement that

supported her, Joan said during the trial the *Chicago Tribune* deemed "The Trial of the Decade," "My life is not in the hands of the court. My life is in the hands of the people." Thousands of people protested, signed petitions, and fundraised on her behalf, resulting in her acquittal and trail-blazing policy changes that continue to impact lives today. Coalitions and partnerships between activist groups like prison abolitionist groups, National Organization for Women, National Association for the Advancement of Colored People, *Ms. Magazine*, American Civil Liberties Union, and musical artists like Sweet Honey and the Rock and many Black women's collectives shared resources and spoke up to demand justice for Joan.

> **'My life is not in the hands of the court. My life is in the hands of the people.'**

Growing up with both Joan's and my mother's stories taught me that our fate is truly in our hands. Systems of domination silence their victims through violence. My cousin's and my mother's stories brought national attention to the intersection of racial and gender justice issues and raised awareness about the power of strong intersectional coalitions and partnerships in fighting for justice.

As my friend and collaborator Courtney Martin so eloquently says, everyone in each of these situations "trusted their own outrage." In the face of oppression, in the face of **gaslighting**, and being deemed oversensitive, race-baiting, or hysterical, they stuck to righteousness.

Collective action is powerful.

The "power with" approach as opposed to a hierarchy of "power over" encourages us to think about solidarity and justice as something beyond allyship. Activists can work together to create narratives, even if they sometimes have differing approaches, to interrupt and disrupt domination. Forcing a space for different theories of change within a system of domination is important and leads to growth.

As a result of my close proximity to this story and my experiences as an organizer in feminist spaces and beyond, I can envision our ability to transcend the clutches of the current system of domination. We must commit to making strategic collaborations that are accessible, accountable, and focused on radical solidarity to truly have justice.

Collective action is powerful.

Standing alongside other young women and carrying the banner leading 2004's million-person March for Women's Lives, was my own rite of passage. It was my time to learn to lead with love and passion and to take the banner forward for the next generation while standing shoulder to shoulder with the women who paved the way for us.

As I marched forward, I flashed-back to a moment when I asked my Mom if I could consider myself "free" since we learned in our elementary school textbooks that slavery in the United States ended in 1865. She answered me with the wisdom of one of her heroes, Fannie Lou Hamer. "Baby, you just need to know one thing when you're doing this work and calling for justice. Do like Fannie said. "Nobody's free until everybody's free."

Now, I think of her teachings when I work to stretch myself in my own march toward justice. We can't rely on the limits of one kind of tactic to get everyone free. We can't prioritize the needs of only the most privileged within our own ranks and think we can achieve justice, equality, dignity, or liberation for the whole.

It is necessary to explore the edges of our strategy, to learn from history and the present and to move forward together with intention, and focus on the most effective solutions emerging from the communities that are directly affected.

'Nobody's free until everybody's free.'

39

WHAT IS JUSTICE?
Who Shapes Justice

We're living in a time where activists, artists, and visionaries have valiantly stepped into an arena with victories that can be the hardest to measure in traditional ways. But we know cultural change and justice when we see it and feel it, and the rewards of progress are always worth it.

Although justice isn't fully determined by what happens in our courts and legal institutions, the decision makers who shape our policies and laws hold power that impacts almost every facet of our lives. By and large, data shows that women's leadership in government and political processes improves them across party lines. Here's a global snapshot of where we are, and it is clear that we have a long way to go to reach parity.[5]

· Did you know that women and gender-nonconforming and nonbinary people are not protected equally by the US Constitution? The Equal Rights Amendment, known as the ERA, is a proposed amendment to the US Constitution aimed at protecting equal legal rights for all American citizens regardless of their sex or gender. Ninety-four percent of Americans support the ERA across political parties and gender identities. In January 2020, Virginia became the thirty-eighth state to ratify the ERA. If the Constitution had been amended to include the ERA, sexual assault survivors like Joan Little would have had these rights to support their cases.

· Women in Rwanda make up 60% of policy makers, 50% of the cabinet, and half of their supreme court justices. Rwanda ranks in the top five countries for gender equity. In contrast, the United States ranks seventy-fifth in the world.

· There are a record 2,276 women —including 552 women of color— US state legislators in 2021. Women will hold 557 state Senate seats (28 percent) and 1,719 state House or Assembly seats (32 percent) — Center for American Progress

28%   32%

· In 2020, a record 220 women Members of Parliament (MPs) were elected in the UK. Women Conservative candidates won eighty-six seats, the most the party has ever had, and more than 50% of Labour MPs are now women. Currently, women make up a third of lawmakers.

· Women account for less than 10% of parliamentarians in single or lower houses in twenty-seven states worldwide, including 3 chambers with zero women represented.—UN Women

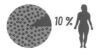

· Eleven women are heads of state and twelve are heads of government.—UN Women

· Only 20.7% of government ministers are women; the top five portfolios most held by women ministers are: social affairs, followed by family/children/youth/elderly/disabled, environment/natural resources/energy, employment/labor/vocational training, and trade/industry.—UN Women

CALL TO ACTION

· *What does justice look and feel like to you?*

· *Take a look at the numbers we've listed here. What do they say to you? How do you want them to change and grow?*

· *What changes would you like to see in your community? What is one step you can take this week to help a cause you care about move forward?*

· *Take a moment to research NGOs and grassroots organizing opportunities in your area? How can you help expand access to political participation for BIPOC, LGBTQIA+, and disabled people in your community? If you can't find one, research an action you can take to plant the seeds of change—this includes starting a petition or organizing like-minded friends to build a campaign.*

"One child, one teacher, one book, one pen can change the world."
—Malala Yousafzai, Nobel Laureate

CHAPTER SIX

Education Equality

"Sit down and read. Educate yourself for the coming conflicts." —
Mother Jones, Irish American humanitarian, labor organizer

"So quick was I at picking up [Chinese] that I was soon able to prompt my brother whenever he got stuck. At this my father used to sigh and say to me: "If only you were a boy how proud and happy I should be." But it was not long before I repented of having thus distinguished myself; for person after person assured me that even boys generally become very unpopular if it is discovered that they are fond of their books. For a girl, of course, it would be even worse."
—Murasaki Shikibu, Japanese novelist

"A good education is another name for happiness."
—Ann Plato, African American and Indigenous American educator and author

"Only that education deserves emphatically to be termed cultivation of mind which teaches young people how to begin to think." — Mary Wollstonecraft, feminist author

GETTING SCHOOLED

What does education mean to you?

For me, faith, family, and education were the sacred trifecta my parents taught me to revere as soon as I could speak each word aloud. I grew up being told that **knowledge is a form of power**. I was told it was especially important for me to honor the legacy of my parents and maternal grandparents who gained higher education while facing barriers as African Americans raised in segregated cities in the southern United States.

Later, when I was a teenager in Saudi Arabia, many American expats were sent home or to Europe to attend boarding schools while their parents remained abroad. I spent one year devoted to preparing for admissions tests, attending school fairs, and touring prospective campuses.

In most cases, the majority of students who both attend and reside at elite private schools are among the most privileged. Since my parents grew up with modest means in segregated schools, I had no lived insight into what my experience would be like as a first-generation Black prep-school attendee. How would I feel? For my parents, segregation laws in the 1960s and the high price of tuition barred them from even considering this option for themselves. Although the landmark ruling that mandated equity in schools passed a decade before my mom was in high school, the deeply entrenched systemic racism within her local and state institutions still prevailed. My mom was selected as one of the first Black students to possibly begin integrating white schools in her community, but she decided to stay at her high school where her father taught math and industrial arts.

Mom often spoke about how double standards about resources, support, materials, and equipment impacted the lives of both Black students and teachers. And most of all, about how a so-called **"separate but equal"** system failed everyone because it prevented all students from experiencing different cultures and gaining insights that exposure to diverse ideas and people can provide. Through her stories, I understood that schools play a huge role in shaping our experience, and mirror the hurdles enshrined in our labor, cultural, political, and legal systems.

Since their employer pledged to support my education abroad as a part of their contract, my parents jumped on the opportunity to send me to a school known for its academic rigor. Because their only instruction was that I select a school that provided me with diverse and comprehensive course options, I was a bit overwhelmed with the possibilities.

When I pored through glossy brochures featuring campuses across the globe, I became overwhelmed by the benefits each school provided. Since every school advertised their scholarly, artistic, and athletic excellence, I tried to read between the lines to work out whether I could truly fit in. Most of the schools I considered were consistently mostly white, mostly wealthy, and mostly suburban environments in the United States and United Kingdom.

To my surprise, gender came up a lot for me throughout my process. I naively assumed I wouldn't have to be as strict about my dress code as I did out in public in Saudi Arabia. During my time in the Kingdom, girls and women expats were required to dress modestly by covering our shoulders and knees in public. We were strongly encouraged to follow the rules by religious police who roamed the streets and the malls at that time to discourage disobedience.

As I flipped through the brochure pages, I asked myself why so many of the school uniforms appeared to infantilize young women, dictating what they should wear. On the other hand, many of the young cis men were dressed in clothes that mirrored the suits they would be expected to wear in their expected high-powered roles in the future. In some of the coeducational schools, I noticed that uniform requirements and expectations were defined across strict binary gender lines, reinforcing the idea that we should all conform to specific gender roles instead of expressing ourselves on our own terms.

After looking through a pile of about twenty advertisements, a bright-blue pamphlet captured my gaze. I read the words on the cover aloud because I was intrigued, "BLUESTOCKINGS."

As I devoured the brochure, I knew that a school started by feminist educators would connect me to a lineage of learning I may not access elsewhere. Although there were a lot of obvious differences between the foremothers of the institution and me, their enduring mission to educate young women and girls with the motto **"Truth without fear"** spoke to me. After all, feminism when upheld and practiced righteously and justly reminds me of that maxim that inspired me to move far away from home and start my learning adventure.

Let's flash forward to when I arrived at my new boarding school. While feminism was something we discussed often due to my school's **first-wave feminist** values, I now wonder what it would have been like if we could have participated in the "feminism-in-schools" movement championed by education leaders like Ileana Jiménez, creator of the #HSfeminism and #K12feminism hashtags, who made waves at the first-ever International Girls' Studies Association Conference in Norwich, United Kingdom, in 2016.

Now that I'm aware of this burgeoning movement of teachers actively integrating feminism into their K–12 curriculum, I wonder what I could have better understood about myself and my community if I had access to intentional intersectional feminist teaching at that time. Even though my courses were informative and inquiry-based, which I loved, I took a lot of weekend trips to college campuses to dig deeper into the complexities of feminism beyond what was included in the formal curriculum.

When I was in school, I learned that University of Bologna graduate Bettisia Gozzadini became the first woman to teach at a university in 1239. In the early 1500s, when women lacked proper legal rights, a select group of women who accessed higher education in patriarchal Europe were not permitted to receive the degrees they earned. I also heard several times that Abigail Adams, the wife of John Adams (the second president of the United States) called on her husband to "remember to think about the Ladies" while he and the other "founding fathers" signed the Declaration of Independence. She argued that within the "new Constitution," women must have both equal legal representation and educational access to "encourage learning and virtue." Influenced by the age of reason and the ascent of individualism, women challenged blocks to higher education for women and secondary education for girls, fair employment opportunities, and discriminatory practices.

Inspired by both the French and American Revolutions, English author Mary Wollstonecraft published her *Thoughts on the Education of Daughters* in 1787 at the age of nineteen, and *A Vindication of the Rights of Woman* in 1792.

I learned in my modern history class that Wollstonecraft's *Vindication of the Rights of Woman* was a response to philosopher Jean-Jacques Rousseau's *Emile*, which reduced women. Wollstonecraft provided an eloquent clapback against limited gender roles and advocacy for women's education, right to free speech, and right to property ownership. In the years that followed in Europe and the United States, what is known as the first wave of recorded and organized feminist resistance continued from the late 1700s through the First World War.

But, even at a feminist school, I needed to go beyond the assigned textbooks. By reading books my Black professor mother gave me, going on outings with my friends to see Black feminist scholar bell hooks address local college students, and attending riot girl shows in the city to get access to insurgent new zines and mixtapes, I sought to discover more about how colonialism, race, gender identity, and sexuality fit into the conversation beyond our assigned textbooks. I also teamed up with other like minds and wrote for the school paper and joined Model United Nations, while infusing these ideas into our debates and discussions.

In spite of all of this, I still yearned for more opportunities to read about, study, and engage with work by and for feminists of color, LGBTQIA+ luminaries, and disabled leaders in the classroom.

Beyond the classroom, I began to learn and understand that different schools of thought exist within feminism. For example, let's look at how these different groups might view education.

Liberal feminist viewpoints might highlight continued challenges with the modern education system due to *some* continued issues with patriarchy, while uplifting specific individual or group advances. Radical feminists would say that the system itself remains deeply flawed and oppressive due to a **patriarchal** origin (created by men for boys). Alternately, socialist feminists would pinpoint economic injustice, corporate power, corruption, and capitalism as the forces responsible for gendered educational disparities. Black feminists and transnational feminists

would argue that sexism, racism, class oppression, gender identity, immigration status, and globalization impact educational equity and are all inextricably bound together. These groups are all under the feminist umbrella, but all with different ideas as to the solutions.

Whilst my feminist education was extremely strong for the mid-to-late 1990s, I ponder what would have happened if I had been exposed to multiple approaches to feminism and debates within the movement in the classroom.

As evidenced by the emergence of a #HSfeminism movement, feminist standpoints on the role of education in society and culture have evolved over time, even before the term itself was devised in 1895—

WOM
POW

WOMEN
UNITE

GRL

PWR

and these varied viewpoints also show up in how different teachers and institutions approach the subject. Today, kindergarten through secondary-school feminist educators actively teach feminism to their students by providing them with tools to understand the world around them using the lenses of justice, equity, human rights, and activism. Their courses provide students with theories to explore that help them understand how gender, race, class, immigration, and other issues impact their lives and others.

Today, instead of studying only one unit or a chapter about the subject itself, feminism is a path for critical thought and discourse within and outside of itself. It is expanding minds and making way for not only more feminist schools but also more feminist movements, arts and athletic spaces, workplaces, and municipalities in the future.

Over twenty years later, when I walk through the halls of the academic building I studied in, I smile at the walls which have the names of global intersectional women leaders etched into stone. I also reflect on what it means that I found out almost twenty years later that the award I won at age seventeen was established by the family of the first Black graduate of my alma mater.

For so many years, I walked with pride from receiving a prize without knowing that I followed in the footsteps of an African American expat, who bravely integrated our school and went on to be a socialist and women's liberation movement leader and writer. I don't think it was a coincidence that both of us were drawn to a place whose vision for feminism inspired us and where our own voices and impact opened minds and doors to new possibilities too. I used to think I was drawn to my school because of its unique feminist history, and later I learned that part of my purpose was to be a part of its feminist evolution.

How are you going to champion feminist education in your school or community?

FOLX! RUN FOR OFFICE!

ABORTION MY BODY, MY CHOICE

EDUCATION EQUALITY STILL MATTERS

Education helps us shape our understanding of ourselves, our communities, and the larger world. Schools set norms and inform our ideas about participation, political power, and shared values in our culture.

Worldwide, students from marginalized genders are often prevented from thriving at school due to experiencing hazardous commutes to school, street harassment, poverty, period stigma, immigration status, and outdated notions about marriage, traditional gender roles, and work.

Depending on where they live, many young women, girls, and nonbinary youth face barriers to safe, quality, and equitable education.

While some significant strides have been made in many educational systems worldwide, inequities in our societies at large continue to be reflected in school policies, coursework, sporting teams, performance arts communities, and more. Moreover, many of the ideas and, sometimes, misconceptions we have about social movements, including feminism, LGBTQIA+ activism, and racial justice, are rooted in biases and obstacles girls, young women, and nonbinary students encounter in schools. According to UNESCO, "Biases against girls run deep in education systems, whether in terms of participation, textbooks, or teachers' attitudes." Studies show that when girls and young women have support and resources to advance their education, they benefit by earning about 20% more in their adult lives per year of school, which also strengthens their communities.

> **"Biases against girls run deep in education systems, whether in terms of participation, textbooks, or teachers' attitudes."**

• Girls are more likely to never enter primary school than boys. —UNICEF

• Most countries have achieved gender equity in primary school enrolment, but in many countries, inequities disadvantaging girls continue. —UNICEF

• 59% of trans students have been blocked from entering restrooms consistent with their gender identity. —National Center for Transgender Equity

• Despite all international and national efforts, over half of children out of school are girls. 31 million girls are still out of school around the world. —UNESCO

• 84% of transgender students and 70% of gender-nonconforming students were bullied or harassed at school. —GLSEN

• Women are underrepresented in tech and scientific disciplines due to social and cultural obstacles to management and leadership roles. Only 29% of the world's researchers are women. —UNESCO

WHY GENDER STUDIES? WHY NOW?

'There is nothing radical about common sense.'

— **Judith Butler**, philosopher, gender studies theorist, author

Gender studies helps us make sense of who we are and how gender, race, sexuality, and class impact our lives, systems, and human experience. Gender studies is an interconnected field that explores gender, sexuality, culture, literature, language, colonialism, power dynamics, labor, societies, and justice.

Gender studies work is usually placed in humanities and social science departments but it has relevance across disciplines. In gender studies courses, students examine social justice, labor issues, global politics, LGBTQIA+ theory and studies, intersectionality, and the history of feminist thought and activism. One of my favorite activities from when I taught my gender studies course to first-years in college was to ask who identified as a feminist on the first day of class. By the end of the course, almost everyone raised their hands because they understood the value of understanding the ideas, history, and norms that shape our society.

Recently, due to the rise of **authoritarian** governance worldwide, scholars in this field have been battling pressure from opponents who attack this logical discipline as 'ideology' instead of science, which is an example of the persistence of gender bias in itself. Anti-trans activists also try to denounce transgender equality by branding it as a '(trans)gender ideology' rather than a pursuit for equality and justice. In the same year that the Hungarian government decided to take away accreditation from gender studies departments, the president of the National Women's Studies Association, Premilla Nadasen disputed the 'gender ideology' claims, as well as the falsehood that gender studies clash with family values. She said, 'Women and gender studies scholars are not rooted in a 'gender ideology.' They think about gender as a frame of analysis for understanding the way in which the world works. I think if there's any ideology that has been manifest in this debate, it's the right-wing ideology that is attempting to return to **heteronormative** patriarchal society.'

SOCIAL
JUSTICE

FEMINIST
HISTORY

ACTIVISM

CALL TO ACTION

• *Take a look at the stats in this section. Did anything surprise you?*

• *Think about a moment when you learned most of your ideas about gender, justice, and equality. How much did you learn about feminism in school? Where else did you get your information? What could have been different in your life if you learned about feminism earlier in life?*

• *Look back at your educational experience up to this point. Who has had the most influence on your perspective about feminism thus far? Your parents? Friends? Media? How did what you learned in school align or conflict with what you heard from other sources?*

• *Take a few minutes to jot down how gender plays a role in dress codes, sports, performance arts, school elections, and social dynamics at your school. Do you see any issues that need to be addressed? What is one step you can take to make your voice heard or help drive change?*

"We still are not paid equally. And if you believe that it's a myth, do the math. Unequal pay hurts women. It hurts their families. And it hurts us all. You and I have to continue fighting for equal pay for equal work. I get up each day with that on my mind, because I need to make a difference." — Lilly Ledbetter, equal pay activist

"In this country, lesbianism is a poverty—as is being brown, as is being a woman, as is being just plain poor. The danger lies in ranking the oppressions. The danger lies in failing to acknowledge the specificity of the oppression. The danger lies in attempting to deal with oppression purely from a theoretical base. Without an emotional, heartfelt grappling with the source of our own oppression, without naming the enemy within ourselves and outside of us, no authentic, non-hierarchical connection among oppressed groups can take place." — Cherríe L. Moraga, Chicana feminist writer and activist

CHAPTER SEVEN

Money

ECONOMIC INJUSTICE

When I was in college, I interned at a global feminist organization based in Washington, DC. On a daily basis, we focused on influencing US trade policy to benefit poor women and girls worldwide. It was there that I learned that gender justice impacts our ability to build the resources we need to thrive in society as both individuals, and as families, and communities.

One day, I was watching Queen Noor of Jordan speak about the connection between economics and gender justice. It was then that it occurred to me that I actively avoided talking about money outside of economics classes at school.

I realized that I carried a lot of shame and uneasiness about speaking up about how money, student debt, and how income insecurity had impacted my loved ones—and therefore my own life.

I was reminded of the time when I asked my parents why some of my private school classmates were given **stock portfolios** as graduation gifts, when I didn't even know what they were. It was then that I began to engage in conversations with relatives

about the impact of the lack of **reparations** for slavery and the generations of wealth stolen from **BIPOC** people in our country, in addition to the extra expenses of living in rural **food deserts** with lengthy commutes added.

Before these discussions, I hadn't even thought of how discriminatory fees like the **tampon tax** (for essential products that only people from marginalized genders use) placed an added burden on women, trans men, and non-binary people of color and our families. In an extended family composed of many single mothers, I also heard about the hardship women breadwinners experienced both in and out of the workplace.

Despite working multiple nonstop jobs and defying the myth of the **American Dream**, I instead witnessed the firsthand truth of Dr. Martin Luther King Jr.'s retort about how BIPOC people are stigmatized and shut out of economic systems that aren't designed for them to thrive in. He said, "It's a cruel jest to say to a bootless man that he ought to lift himself by his bootstraps." Although his words didn't take Black feminist theory into account, which would emerge in the coming years, the "double jeopardy" of being both Black and a woman, as radical Black feminist Flo Kennedy named it, adds to the impact of economic injustice both then and now.

Around that time, I started reading about radical feminist Shulamith Firestone. She wrote about a utopian society without the oppression of women. Firestone believed that the class of men and the class of women led to women's marginalization in society. She summed up that freeing women from pressures to have children would allow for more equitable engagement in the workforce and more autonomy. In her assessment, women who worked at home without pay for their impactful and meaningful domestic labor helped fuel the capitalist economy for men to dominate the public sphere. Although I personally wasn't in alignment with *all* of Shulamith's views, she expanded my mind about how to value the labor we so often aren't compensated for because it is minimized and stigmatized as "women's work."

I realized that it was born from recognizing that power, privilege, gender, and racial inequality played a role in shaping my access to a living wage in spite of the faux **meritocracy** we were raised to believe in at school and in the media. While watching a panel of mostly wealthy experts talk about economic injustice, I imagined what it would be like to speak about my own experiences with sexual harassment from customers while waiting tables for measly tips, or asking relatives to tell the truth about horrific experiences in low-wage, discriminatory, and sometimes unsafe factory, care-taking, and domestic work environments.

'It's a cruel jest to say to a bootless man that he ought to lift himself by his bootstraps.'

It was in that moment in an internship that paid me about $8 an hour (one of the only college internships a middle-class student like myself could afford to do without parental help because it was not unpaid) that I became determined to learn more. As I showed up for work every day to do data entry work about the status of gender and economics worldwide, I pledged to act and speak up more about the realities of how historic and systemic injustice had an economic impact on my life and others.

THE NUMBER$ DON'T LIE

• Worldwide, men are more likely to earn more than women.

• Indigenous American women only make 58 cents on the dollar compared to white men. For a population of women who are murdered at rates 10 times the national average, the pay gap is a matter of life and death. —NBC

• Black women experience a wage gap at every education level, and the gap is largest for the most educated Black women.—NWLC

• In the US it is increasingly common for women to be the primary earner in their families, with most relying on breadwinning mothers for the majority of their earnings. — Institute for Women's Policy Research

• On average, LGBTQIA+ couples raising families make 20% less than heterosexual couples in the United States, and are more likely to live in poverty.

• Fair property inheritance systems are becoming more commonplace in recent years. But men tend to own more land and assets than women across the globe.

• Fifteen percent of transgender folks live at a poverty rate that is nearly four times that of the general population. LGBTQIA+ BIPOC families experience the worst of the disparities. —American Progress

• The UK government announced in the 2020 Budget that the "tampon tax" of 5% Value Added Tax will finally be scrapped. In 2014, Laura Coryton launched a petition after discovering that Jaffa cakes, crocodile steaks, and private jet maintenance aren't classed by Her Majesty's Revenue and Customs as nonessential luxury items under VAT rules— but tampons were.

CALL TO ACTION

"Feminist philanthropy is not a charitable act or an act of power. It is an act of solidarity and mutual empowerment, in which the solutions to the problems that women face are seen as a matter of mutual responsibility." —Fondo Centroamericano de Mujeres (Nicaraguan Women's Fund)

• 2020 was slated to be the year when freedom fighter and American abolitionist, Harriet Tubman's face would change the face of US currency when the Obama administration announced this shift in 2016. The Trump administration decided to delay the process of replacing former president Andrew Jackson's visage on our currency by calling it "pure political correctness." Have you ever looked at your money and asked yourself what story it tells you about who your country values? Write down what thoughts come up for you. Consider starting a petition campaign like the one that led to Tubman's selection for the $20 bill in your community. Whose face would you like to see on currency?

• In 2018, Iceland became the first country to hold companies accountable for paying people equally by requiring them to demonstrate their practices. What do you know about equal pay laws in your country? Do you know if the school you attend pays your teachers, administrators, and other laborers equally?

• Do you want to help resource feminist work? While we most often associate the word "philanthropy" with the act of an individual or institution donating to a cause, the true meaning of the word is "love of humankind. " FRIDA: The Young Feminist Fund and the Third Wave Fund are feminist activist funds that are run by and for young women of color, and LGBTQIA+ folks. If you have resources to contribute, consider donating to both funds. Or, perhaps you have a movement you're organizing that could use support. Visit both funds for information about how to get involved with them and their grantees.

"When I dare to be powerful, to use my strength in the service of my vision, then it becomes less and less important whether I am afraid."
—Audre Lorde, writer and activist, self-described "Black, lesbian, mother, warrior, poet"

CHAPTER EIGHT

Power

"Let's be gentle with ourselves and each other and fierce as we fight oppression."
—Dean Spade, activist, writer, teacher

"If knowledge is power, power is also knowledge, and a large factor in their subordinate position is the fairly systematic ignorance patriarchy imposes upon women."
—Kate Millett, writer

"I believe in my power. I believe in your power. I believe in our power."
—Raquel Willis, writer, and activist

"The value of my life had been obliterated as much by being female as by being Black and poor. Racism and sexism in America were equal partners in my oppression." —Elaine Brown, author, and activist

A STORY OF POWER

Books are my love language. For as long as I can remember, my mom started the tradition of writing me letters, inspiring me with big ideas, and sharing her favorite freedom songs within the margins of children's books, poetry collections, memoirs, anthologies, scholarly texts, and even business guides. To this day, copies of *Sister Outsider* by Audre Lorde, *Daughter of Destiny* by Benazir Bhutto, *Letter to My Daughter* by Maya Angelou, and almost every book written by Alice Walker line my shelf with her eternal notes of guidance and inspiration. Throughout my life, this practice sparked a tradition.

As soon as I could write on my own, I adopted Mom's ritual by writing lengthy tomes back to her and all of my loved ones, family, friends, dogs, ancestors, and even notes to long-departed heroes I'd never

met, including the writer Anne Frank. I also began collecting my favorite feminist texts in secondhand and rare bookstores and chose the copies with personal notes etched inside. My passion for sharing stories as a form of caregiving and affirmation for my community is so deep that whenever I am asked what I want as a gift, I ask for books with notes and wisdom inscribed within them.

One example of this happened on the last day of high school. I'll never forget the moment when Hannah, one of my classmates, drove past me to track me down before the last summer break before college. With long flaxen hair flying in the wind, she stuck her head out of her car window and brandished a book in my direction while calling my name.

She handed me the book saying, "Read the note inside, see you at graduation." I looked at the cover of the book in my hand and realized I'd been given a copy of *A Taste of Power: A Black Woman's Story* by Elaine Brown.

I wiped back tears as I read my friend's note about her confidence in my courage, voice, and power now and into the future. She mentioned that she was reminded of me as

JAMIA!

READ THE NOTE INSIDE

she read about Elaine Brown's evolution after attending a mostly white school for "gifted young women" to her experience as a trailblazing Black Panther leader, political activist, and eventual self-described feminist who spoke truth to power in a cis male-dominated organization.

Hannah's gift made me feel seen and heard. During our last few years on campus, I stood for my principles as co-head of our Black Student Union when some white parents took issue with us self-defining the school-sanctioned "Black Awareness Club" with a more powerful, movement-oriented, and activist name. During that same time, we were strongly encouraged by other authority figures on campus to shift our emergent LGBTQIA+, non-Christian (in a Christian-affiliated school), and BIPOC groups to a more sanitized "Diversity Club" umbrella that by its nature decentered the work we were each doing to focus on our specific needs.

When we proposed having each specific affinity group exist independently under a broader coalition, we encountered some obstacles because it went against the widely accepted

"color-blind" framework of the time. Instead of accepting what we were told was a more suitable and less "controversial" way to address our concerns about imbalanced power, we chose to amplify how the inequities of the outside world still penetrated the hallowed walls of our otherwise progressive school.

When Hannah handed me *A Taste of Power* the night before I was slated to address the student body as our elected class speaker, I knew that it was a reminder to step into my power and own my voice. As I walked up to the podium the next day, I decided to forgo the lion's share of what I had written in the document our headmistress asked to review and approve beforehand.

Instead, with shaking ankles (thank goodness for the long

"DIVERSITY CLUB"

gown!) and a bold voice, I decided to speak about what I had learned about standing up for one's values even when you are outnumbered. I shared what I'd gathered from the students who stood with me and others in solidarity when their power and privilege could have made the alternative more convenient. I spoke about what it meant to study books about defiance, justice, and even antiheroes who chose to see, speak, imagine, and hold power differently and to use that to try to remake the world.

As I walked back to my seat, I basked in the energy of the moment. I wanted to memorize the power I'd gained in seeing myself as a leader for the first time. I spoke and lived out loud what I know in my bones, which is that it is up to us to define ourselves or someone else will. By unearthing and examining our own stories and learning from the stories of others—and especially those who are overtly or covertly pushed to the margins and silenced, we speak truth to power. We remind ourselves and each other that true power has nothing to do with dominance, supremacy,

rule, or control. Instead, power has everything to do with collaboration, community action, empathy, listening, and freedom with no one left behind.

Hannah's simple gesture lit a fire within me. It reminded me of my courage by sharing someone else's story through a book. As I left campus to take on college and the rest of my life, I thought about how my activism started on the playground when I called out bullies for using racial and anti-Semitic slurs. Over time, I lived up to my nickname "Rebel with a Cause," with bumps, scrapes, and sometimes a foot in my mouth along the way. This same spirit led me to participate in my first racial justice protest at the age of ten with my parents. In middle school and high school, I ran for student council, set up recycling campaigns, and passed petitions to fight apartheid in South Africa and to free political prisoners around the world.

The late, great Black feminist firebrand Florynce "Flo" Kennedy said, "The biggest sin is sitting on your ass…. Don't agonize. Organize." Her "verbal karate" as feminist activist

'The biggest sin is sitting on your ass... Don't agonize. Organize.'

Gloria Steinem described her organizing superpowers, still informs movement battle cries worldwide. The works of activist writers, filmmakers, and artists can remind us of our own power, gifts, and ability to make change. Art and books can also provide us a road map for the future and help us avoid repeating mistakes from the past.

At the time, I didn't realize that the lessons I was learning about the power of the collective were just as meaningful as the power I would have to wait to hold as a voter when I turned eighteen. And when I did turn eighteen, and my **absentee vote** was cast and likely miscounted in a highly contested election fraught with voter suppression against marginalized communities like mine, I knew I had to flex the power of my voice, my pen, and my shoe leather to canvas for changes in a system in need of a complete transformation.

When I think of the people-power that will define this generation, I think of marriage equality; Occupy Wall Street; the United State's first Black president; our first woman presidential popular vote winner in the United States; thousands of anti-deportation and travel ban airport protests; the record-breaking Women's March across seven continents (including Antarctica); Black Lives Matter; Jacinda Ardern, the world's youngest living Prime Minister; and more. I am reminded that the different types of power we need to learn to unpack, examine, build, and reclaim are necessary for us to make a difference in our lives, in those whose futures will be determined by the decisions we made yesterday, and in those we have the power to create with moral intention and action today.

POWER IN NUMBERS
DATA MATTERS.

"There is power in who gets counted, by whom."
—Marcia Douglas, author

Government
According to the Council on Foreign Relations, nineteen out of 193 countries have women heads of state or government. Fourteen out of 193 countries have at least 50% of women in the national cabinet. Four out of 193 countries have at least 50% of women in the national legislature.

Literature
According to VIDA Lit, during this decade, *Harpers Magazine* has published nearly twice as many men as women. *Harper's* has published only six nonbinary writers out of a total of 2,273. The *New York Review of Books* published only 33.37% of women writers. The *London Review of Books* published 32.6% women, with the *Atlantic* publishing 36.55% women and the *Nation* publishing only 39.85% women in their most recent survey. For the first time in almost a decade, *New York Times Book Review* published more than 50% women and *Poetry* published 47.11% women and only 4.59% nonbinary writers.

Media
• The American Society of News Editors' latest tally found that women comprised 41.7% and people of color 22.6% of the overall workforce in newsrooms that responded (17.3%). —The Women's Media Center

• Twenty-eight female journalists in the US and forty-seven of their peers in four other countries report that online abusers directed inappropriate comments, solicitations, and rape threats against them, according to the University of Texas Center for Media Engagement. —The Women's Media Center

• Pay gaps persist along gender lines in newsrooms at the *Associated Press*, the *Los Angeles Times*, the *New York Times*, the *San Francisco Chronicle*, the *Wall Street Journal*, and the *Washington Post*, with men earning substantially more than women. —The Women's Media Center

• Pew Research Center reports that the overall percentage of white and cis male workers in newsrooms is higher than in that of the overall U.S. workforce. —The Women's Media Center

Online

• To fully understand the violent and silencing impact of online abuse on freedom of speech and expression, we need intersectional data. A study by Pew found that fully 25% of young women have been sexually harassed online and 26% have experienced stalking. Moreover, Pew found that women overall are disproportionately targeted by the most severe forms of online abuse, including doxing and violent threats.

Music

• Only 21.7% of artists who put out the top 700 songs since 2012 were women. There is a gender ratio of 4.8 male artists to every one female artist. Male performers were 52% non-white, while 73% of female performers were women of color. —University of Southern California Annenberg Inclusion Initiative

CALL TO ACTION

• *What was the story you grew up hearing about power? How do you feel about it? Who is included, and who is left out? How would you like to rewrite it today?*
• *Who might you give a copy of this book to with a note in the margin? Who would you like to give another book to with a special powerful note to help them tap into their own ability to make change?*
• *What does power mean to you?*
• *When was the first time you felt powerful? Why?*
• *What conditions would need to be present for you to feel more powerful? How can you share your power with others to build power for your community?*
• *What industries are you interested in? What are the numbers? Were they easy to find with a little bit of internet research? If not, how might you lobby to start counting them or begin a tracking or accountability campaign?*

"I've spent so much of my life measuring my quality of life not by my acceptance of my disability, but the erasure of it." —Sarah Michael Hollenbeck, writer and feminist bookstore owner

CHAPTER NINE

Health

On giving birth to her daughter in a New York public clinic in 1970: "I was the only white patient at the clinic. They induced my labor because it was late in the evening and the doctor wanted to go home. I was enraged. The experience made me a feminist." —Barbara Ehrenreich, author and activist

"Health care as a human right, it means that every child, no matter where you are born, should have access to a college or trade-school education if they so choose it, and I think no person should be homeless if we can have public structures and public policy to allow for people to have homes and food and lead a dignified life." —Alexandria Ocasio-Cortez, youngest US Congresswoman

"Inspired by my second-wave feminist mother's battered copy of *Our Bodies, Ourselves*, I set out to gather a group of authors and volunteers who could create the same kind of comprehensive community resource, by and for transgender people, that had been created by the Boston Women's Health Collective." —Dr. Laura Erickson-Schroth, medical doctor and editor, *Trans Bodies, Trans Selves*

"Institutionalized racism prevents us from getting the proper access to health-care services that we need, all the way from before birth. Institutionalized racism continues to tell us that we are not important, we are not powerful people, we are less than, we always have to try harder than everybody else, we have to fight harder, we have to do more. These are barriers. But in spite of those barriers, we are moving past them and we are moving on as a group of people who are moving up to the forefront, right where we belong."—Byllye Avery, health-care leader

A VISION OF HEALTH

When I was about three years old, my right eye was diagnosed with an underdeveloped optic nerve and poor muscle movement. Shortly after, I was declared legally blind in one eye. Many years and stressful doctor's appointments later, I learned that I was born with a congenital cataract and would need multiple surgeries.

Even today, my left eye remains mostly strong, but my right one can make out only shapes, colors, and brightness and has a blind spot on one side despite my cataract removal. That eye has been breaking my heart open ever since my family was told that it was "abnormal." In a world built for people with 20/20 vision, I navigated the world with a different point of view. While I understood that nothing needed to be "fixed" for me to feel whole, worthy, or intact, it didn't help when I began to face misunderstandings, prejudices, and real institutional obstacles as a result of my disability.

My anxieties intensified when I started school, and people started asking me about my eye, which crosses slightly (especially when it's tired). My stomach would twist and turn when other kids commented on my "cross-eyes" and the very fashionable accessories that I had been prescribed for them. There were the eye patches I was supposed to wear at all times to strengthen my sight—one in black that I felt made me look like a child pirate and one ghastly "nude" version designed for white skin that resembled a Band-Aid and clashed with my dark-brown skin—and a much-hated pair of thick-rimmed bubblegum-pink glasses. It was not a cute look, a fact I didn't need to be reminded of by my classmates.

I was supported and cared for at home, but my overachieving family feared the appearance of laziness more than bullying. The main instruction they gave me about my eyes was not to use them as an excuse not to excel. Through observation, I mimicked **hypervigilance** as a survival technique, which, as I am now aware, commonly emerges from experiencing the trauma of systemic injustice, including ableism, racism, heterosexism, transphobia, and sizeism. Due to stigma, shame, and tangible fears about obstacles to equity, I pushed myself constantly to work extra-hard at everything I did, even when it was time to rest or ask for help.

Based on messages I heard at home and what I absorbed in the media, my impulse was like what Olivia Pope's father says to her on one of my favorite shows to stream, *Scandal*: "You have to be twice as good as them to get half of what they have," if you're a Black woman—or in my case, a Black woman with a disability—who wants to be successful in a world that isn't always receptive to you.

I studied for inhuman hours and still received less-than-stellar grades in geometry instead of confessing that it took me longer than most people to read math problems, and I regarded every mistake or average mark as a sign of defeat. When I did well at my work, well-meaning family members or teachers often made comments like, "Wow, look at all you've done with [insert whatever academic achievement here]. Just imagine what you could do with two perfect eyes," not knowing I was tormented by that very idea—that I was missing something.

> **'You have to be twice as good as them to get half of what they have'**

I rarely wore my everyday glasses, which to me were big, ugly reminders of my difference from other people, but despite my best efforts, I couldn't ignore my **monocularity** into nonexistence. I felt incapacitating shame whenever I bumped into a wall I didn't see, walked into a stranger on the street, or missed a detail on an assignment because I was too embarrassed to admit that I couldn't see the board. I couldn't tell the difference between acknowledging the reality of my experience and "not trying hard enough."

During that time, I recognized that I had a complicated relationship with my body and my too frequent experiences with mostly cis male and mostly white health-care workers who often undermined my voice when I spoke about the pain I experienced and its effect on my life. Although I put on a brave and unfettered face with friends and family, I found solace in books created in the feminist health movement, also known as the women's health movement, of the 1960s–1980s.

I finally confided in my mother that I connected my body with betrayal due to both my eye and an agonizing menstrual disorder called endometriosis (one that my cis male doctor characterized as "mild"). She introduced me to books like Boston Health Collective's *Our Bodies, Ourselves* and pamphlets from Planned Parenthood's teen program and the Black Women's Health Project to guide me toward increased understanding and connection to my own body and the shared experiences of others. In addition to gifting me with technical books and resources, she took me to deaf rights movement events with colleagues from her work as a speech pathologist and filled my shelves with books by womanist author, Alice Walker to help me celebrate and appreciate the diversity of the disability community I didn't fully count myself in—yet.

Mom shared that Walker was included on "Mama's syllabus" because she wanted me to know and connect with the story of another southern-born Black woman whose experience of being blind in one eye shaped her understanding of her own worth and value in the midst of race, class, and gender injustice in our culture. Most of all, she wanted me to know how these experiences impacted Walker's writing and ability to "see" the world with a visionary feminist perspective.

Little did I know, long before I'd find my first "Endo Warriors" Facebook group or my first online message board about my visual condition, Mom used the feminist frameworks of self-determination, **consciousness raising**, and respect for bodily autonomy to guide me to a healthier place.

Although she didn't use many words, she understood what I was going through and wanted to share the tools that helped her understand that she was a part of a shared experience, and that her body wasn't the problem, the unjust system that made her feel othered or "less than" was at fault.

Despite this self-reflection, many years of denial came at a high cost. In college, I would respond with clipped matter-of-factness when a new roommate would curiously ask me why my eye would get lazy before bed and would only ever address my disability when I was forced to appeal for extra time on tests. After graduating, I continued to downplay the issue as best I could. Then, finally, several years ago, after absorbing decades of stress, my body waged a full mutiny: all at once, I was overcome with physical fatigue, food allergies, autoimmune breakdown, gastrointestinal distress, and beyond. Alarmingly, the vision in my "good" eye

began to diminish. I was forced to take a break. Not that it was easy: it was humbling and terrifying to be late with deadlines or to bail on meetups with friends for the first time in my life. Plus, I had also killed my ability to simply BE by DOING way too much for way too long. It was time to examine the power dynamics of a system and culture that would define my worth by my capacity to produce and be "fit" and "strong" instead of honoring my inborn value.

This was the wake-up call I needed to finally go see a doctor, after dodging visits whenever possible for almost thirty years. The first one I saw confirmed everything I disliked about those visits. Among other tremendously callous moves, he said that someone with my condition didn't deserve the extra time on standardized tests that I need to do well. Apparently, giving someone like me extra privileges just because I only have one functional eye isn't fair to people with "REAL learning disabilities," as he put it. My heart smarted from making myself so vulnerable just to have my insecurities thrown in my face. It made me feel exactly as I had in high school when I overworked myself in order to be "perfect" without realizing I was eating away at the life force I needed to see my ambitions through. I eventually found a doctor who treated me with humanity and kindness, but more than that, I finally found it in myself to begin to come to terms with my disability.

Microaggressions can feel like a million little paper cuts that compound themselves into ugly scars with a lingering itch. But, once I was able to move past the sluggishness of stigma, I embraced my disability as one of my many identities that informs my life. Feminism, like disability, is not a dirty word, yet it has been referred to many times as the "other F word" due to stigma. Now, when I fear the clutches of stigma's talons, I picture a flashback of myself dancing the night away at a 2004 Planned Parenthood fundraiser headlined by the iconic rock singer Joan Jett while she sang "I don't give a damn about my bad reputation, you're living in the past, it's a new generation." This was just

an hour after being yelled at for being an "angry man-hating feminist" as one of the young people carrying the banner at the million-person-strong March for Women's Lives protest in Washington, DC.

'I don't give a damn about my bad reputation, you're living in the past, it's a new generation.'

Despite the words of our naysayers attempting to diminish us with their screams, in that moment, I was mighty. I wanted everyone who had ever made fun of my eye to see me moving forward in a mass of other bodies with all of their scars and other stories etched into their skin and memory. There, I was tethered to the voices and stories of countless names and faces who marched for reproductive justice and the comprehensive health care they deserved in all the varied shapes and forms they showed up in.

Call to Action

Is feminism good for your health? Take a moment to journal about the following health-care scenarios and considerations.

· **The Politics of Pain:** Did you know that women are more likely to have chronic pain, are less likely to be provided effective pain management than cis men, and statistically less likely to be taken as seriously in the emergency rooms in hospitals? Studies show that Black patients were 40% less likely to receive medication to ease acute pain and Latinx patients were 25% less likely to receive effective pain treatment compared to white patients in emergency rooms. [American Journal of Emergency Medicine] Do you have any personal experiences with pain bias? Why do you think pain experienced by people with marginalized gender, racial, and class identities is more common and more often ignored?

· **COVID-19 Outbreak:** Why do you think initial efforts to address COVID-19 were more successful in nations led by women, including New Zealand, Finland, and Germany? How do you think the ideology of toxic masculinity impacted how the coronavirus was handled in countries with gender disparities in government? In 2020, the mostly elderly and male members of the Academie Francaise that provides guidance about the usage of French language encouraged people to stop referring to COVID-19 using masculine articles, and deemed the coronavirus feminine. What do you think of this? How does language (in any tongue) inform how we think about health and our relationship to it?

· **Health Care Is A Human Right:** Is health care (all health care, including reproductive health care for people of all genders, ages, and abilities) treated as a human right in your country? If so, do you know how accessible comprehensive, age-appropriate health care is for the most vulnerable and marginalized people in your community? Who is left behind within the health-care system you're currently in? Who benefits from this structure? What is your vision for how health care should be given and treated worldwide? What could schools do to offer better and more meaningful health care to make everyone feel included and supported?

"Caring for myself is not self-indulgence, it is self-preservation, and that is an act of political warfare." —Audre Lorde, feminist and womanist author, librarian, and activist

CHAPTER TEN

Wellness

On how activism has transformed since the 1960s and 1970s: "Self-care has to be incorporated in all of our efforts. And this is something new. This holisti approach to organizing is wha is going to eventually move u along the trajectory that may lead to some victories." — Angela Davis, activist, philosopher, and scholar

"You've been taught to be obedient. Not how to activate healing in therapy." — Dr. Jennifer Mullan, therapist and founder of Decolonizing Therapy

"Please prioritize your self-care as you move through this work. Do not use it as an excuse to not do the work in a substantial way, but at the same time, honor yourself and the different feelings that show up around your identities." —Layla Saad, anti-racist author, speaker and teacher

"I am learning to engage in generative conflict, to say no, to feel my limits, taking time to feel my heartache when it comes— from living in America, from interpersonal trauma or grief, from movement losses." — Adrienne Maree Brown, author and pleasure activist

THE MAGIC FIX

What does the word "wellness" mean to you? Many people understand wellness as a simple state of being well, safe, and thriving in body, mind, and spirit. For others, wellness is defined by individuals making personal choices to take care of themselves without the influence of others or outside factors. In a world where we're constantly told we need to "detox" our bodies as if they were inherently toxic, "clean up" our eating as if nourishing ourselves is somehow dirty, or silence our true feelings and mask them with solely "positive" words and thoughts, it is important for us to unpack and understand what being well and cared for looks and feels like for us.

Depending on who you are, your culture, and how your identity relates to power and privilege in your community, the political nature of these words may feel muted, charged, or somewhere in between. I'm a longtime participant in the wellness movement as one of the many women, girls, and nonbinary people living with chronic conditions that haven't been adequately addressed by the mainstream medical establishment. Like many others, my quest for deeper empathy, nurturing, and compassionate comprehensive care led me to seek alternative means to support the treatments I received in many medical settings where my pain or concerns about the documented link between race, economic status, and gender were not taken seriously enough.

RELAX

FREE YOUR BODY AND MIND

In a climate rife with corporate "women's empowerment" or faux feminist wellness campaigns, "wellness" is often sold as a product or ideal that individuals can obtain if they possess the resources to be more "successful" humans. Hence it is important for us to be able to discern what products, messages, and services truly help and which ones deepen the hurt we're already experiencing. Thankfully, intersectional feminism provides us with the theories we need to help us build our own understanding of wellness and consider what kind of support we need and why in a pressure cooker of a culture and health-care system that has a long way to go to be inclusive, protective, and supportive of everyone who needs care and dis/ability accommodations.

Too often, the advertisements we scroll through on Instagram and TikTok, read at the bus stop, or hear on podcasts reinforce the idea that happiness, healing, and health are something we can achieve if we work harder, spend more money, deprive ourselves of nourishment, think and speak only positive thoughts, or "fake it until we make it." These messages are so commonplace that we begin to perceive ourselves as problems needing solving, instead of people living in a world that needs to be transformed with food, environmental justice, education, comprehensive health care access, and equity at all levels.

As I began to read and learn more about feminism, I began to understand that both self-care and community care are essential to our work and our lives. Although my journey with this concept began long ago, it was underscored during a gathering of intersectional feminists at the City University of New York in 2019.

When I joined Glory Edim, creator of the Well-Read Black Girl book club, anthology, and festival, and black feminist scholars Alexis Pauline Gumbs, Christen Smith, and Bianca Williams for a conversation about "Agency + Care: The Power of Black Women Reading," I didn't expect that our conversation would linger in my mind for months. When I reflect back on it now, it was a form of medicine or a salve that helped me think about and prioritize the power of personal and community wellness in new and mighty ways.

In a discussion about how authors including Octavia Butler, Toni Morrison, and Claudia Rankine inspired us as readers, writers, activists, and truth-tellers through their visionary books and wisdom, we celebrated how the practice and lineage of Black Women's writing and consciousness raising provided us with experiences of both self-care and community care through being reflected on the page in a world where our stories are often silenced, undermined, or pushed to the margins.

Although our multigenerational gathering took place in the university building where I worked, members of the public participated in our conversation and gathered with us in a circle of shared storytelling.

After we engaged in a lively dialogue about how gaining insight into the lives and work of Black women educators, creators, and seekers helped us set our sights on and attempt to pave our way toward a more inclusive and just future, we opened up the conversation to discuss why the power of reading individually and communally was so therapeutic for Black trans and cis folks in a publishing landscape where only 5% of the industry is black.

As we poured ourselves into the discussion, we celebrated the endurance of our ancestors while lamenting the trials they encountered as Black authors, creators, and scholars within structures hell-bent on suppressing their voices and squelching their power.

Following what felt like a triumphant group roll call of the trailblazing women of color leaders who graced the building we were in many years before, an audience member stood up and faced us panelists on the dais.

I'll never forget the loving but haunting words she shared while pointing at beautiful collages Alexis Pauline Gumbs made in tribute to our late literary foreparents Audre Lorde, June Jordan, Octavia Butler, and Lorraine Hansberry.

As she pulled a few tendrils of her long jet-black dreadlocks behind her ears, she said with concern, "It is beautiful that we're celebrating the loves of these powerful ancestors. But we must ask ourselves why it is that none of them made it to their seventieth birthdays. What can we do, knowing that the systems we're in are not created for us to thrive or even survive as Audre Lorde told us, to ensure that each of you and us are cared for, supported, and protected now and into the future?" After what felt like a bellowing silence, the air in the room stiffened before we could exhale. My palms were sweaty as I thought of my Mom who was born during the same era as many of my sheroes and passed away too soon from a cancer that kills women of color and especially Black women at alarming and unrelenting rates.

Suddenly, the room roared with the echoes of affirmation. Many people spoke at once in a chorus as they all blended together into one voice: "Yes, sister. Yes, thank you for caring for and loving us. This is what we're fighting for, for us to be

> '**It is beautiful that we're celebrating the lives of these powerful ancestors. But we must ask ourselves why it is that none of them made it to their seventieth birthdays.**'

here and for a world where you can and will live a long and abundant life too. Thank you for reminding us why we're here."

In a culture that attempts to sell us products masked as magic fixes to the structures that limit our open and equal participation in the workplace, media, politics, and more, her message cut like a saber. The searing truth of her words bore into me, reminding me of the way former Black Panther Assata Shakur's soaked into my skin when I read them in high school.

> **"It is our duty to fight for our freedom. It is our duty to win. We must love each other and support each other. We have nothing to lose but our chains."**

REAL TALK: GET A SHRINK TO FIT
Fight Stigma and Find Support

Have you ever felt like you were living in a house of mirrors? My second year of college was one of the most stressful times of my life. I had a nightmare of a breakup and developed severe and chronic health issues; meanwhile I was in school full time and working two jobs.

Although I was known for usually being a cheerful and upbeat person, I felt like I was constantly carrying a bag of bricks on my back. I lost twenty pounds that year, and not intentionally. I didn't stop going to my classes, but any time I wasn't studying or at work, I was either crying or sleeping.

On top of all that, I felt horribly guilty for being unhappy because I had the privilege of living in a safe and beautiful university environment. At the time, I didn't connect how the sexist and racist pressures of the "superwoman" and "strong black woman" tropes I was often urged to conform to were eating away at my insides. At first, I tried talking to my friends and family about how I was feeling, but they quickly grew frustrated with my endless distress and the fact that none of their advice or admonishments seemed to help, so I stopped mentioning my sadness to anyone, and withdrew deeper into the dark hole in my heart.

I tried a bunch of things that people had told me would help: exercise, meditation, prayer, self-help books, herbal supplements, etc. Nothing worked. The only relief I got was sleep because at least when I was unconscious, I didn't have to feel anything.

When I woke up one winter day to find that I'd slept for fourteen hours, through an entire day of classes, I realized things had gotten really bad. Desperate, I talked to my prefect about my situation. He recommended I contact the school's counseling center.

Now, I was raised by a father who believed that therapy was only for people with "serious issues" (e.g., a personality disorder or getting over major trauma and abuse). He, like many African American men of his generation, stigmatized mental health care (for a variety of reasons.) He grew up in the segregated American South, in a society that saw Black people as mentally inferior, so the pressure was high to present himself as competent, strong, and lacking problems. He taught me to be resilient, at all costs, in the face of adversity. He would always call on me to tap into my sense of "grit," resulting in my enduring hatred of the word or its mention.

Mental illness, to my father, was a character flaw—a sign of weakness. When I mentioned my stress and sadness to him, he told me I was "oversensitive" and that my issues were "luxury problems." He encouraged me to increase my church attendance, count my blessings, and toughen up. At worst, I'd be called "hysterical" for rejecting these kinds of minimizing remarks, fifty years after the American Medical Association dropped the term, which had been used to pathologize womanhood since 1900 BC.

At times, although he had the best intentions, Dad would ask me what I was doing to cause the problems in my life, that were often systemic. Later, when I heard his mother (my paternal grandmother) say something similar, I realized that so much of this kind of rhetoric is passed down without a thought about the kind of shrapnel these unempathetic words can become in someone else's mind and spirit.

So, when my prefect suggested I talk to a therapist, I told him that I wasn't "crazy," I was just "experiencing a temporary human setback," and I didn't appreciate his pathologizing my situation, which was just stress, not "depression." He quietly wrote the number of the counselor on a Post-it, stuck it on my desk, and left the room.

I spent the next hour staring at the number, weighing the pros and cons of therapy. Finally, it dawned on me that prayer and "sucking it up" were obviously not working for me, and that this was the only option left. I heard these words in my head: this pain can stop now, just call—and I did. I started to feel a little better as soon as I'd made the appointment. I decided to do something  for myself that went against everything I had ever been taught. It was one of the first "adult" decisions that I'd made on my own terms, and I was proud of myself for making it. This was my first step toward feeling like myself again.

When I arrived at the counseling center, I was nervous. I glanced around the room, and when I noticed someone from my French class, I almost ran out. But then my name was called, and I was walked to the therapist's office. The first thing I look at in any room is the bookshelves, and I noticed that hers held books on feminism and on diversity in higher education, which gave me some confidence. Then the therapist just asked, "How are you feeling?" And for the first time, I felt like I didn't have to answer with my usual, "Fine, thanks," but instead could tell someone what was REALLY going on.

The rest of her questions were similarly simple, open-ended, nonjudgmental: "How does that make you feel?" "What makes you feel supported?" "What would feeling better look and feel like for you?" These were things I hadn't even asked myself, and answering them in that office put me in touch with thoughts and feelings I'd been bottling up for a year. Unlike friends and family tend to do, she didn't respond with advice or reprimands but just acknowledged my experiences with compassion. Instead of trying to solve my problems, she listened to me. It was incredibly empowering. It has been a decade since I met my first therapist at the campus center. I'm sad to say that I don't even remember her name today. She armed me with the tools I needed to set stronger boundaries in my relationships and develop healthy ways of coping with stress.

Through therapy, I learned to acknowledge that depression, anxiety, and mental distress are real and that we are all entitled to health care for them just as we would be for any health issue. If you find yourself wondering if you "deserve" to go to a therapist or if your problems are "bad enough" to give you that right, ask yourself if you'd wonder those same things if you broke your ankle or had bronchitis.

I tend to look up intersectional "feminist therapists" who subscribe to a more holistic, relational, and contextual approach. Feminist therapists examine power inside and outside of the therapy relationship. They also acknowledge how patriarchy, classism, and racism have shaped their industry and influenced diagnoses and methods.

Feminist therapy emerged out of the second-wave movement as an approach driven by the "personal is political" adage. I've found feminist therapists I've liked by searching for providers in my area with backgrounds in spirituality, art therapy, and working with former expats, and communities of color. I have also helped friends and family research therapists who specifically specialize in supporting LGBTQIA+ folks, people of faith, refugees, people with trauma, people with disabilities, and transracial adoptees.

While it may take some time to find your perfect match, there is someone out there who can help you, who will support you without **gaslighting** you, mis-gendering you, or lobbing racist microaggressions, and it is worth taking the time and effort to find someone who "gets" and supports you just as you are.

If I had my way, everyone would get free access to intersectional therapy anytime they want it! If you don't have free health care, take a good look at your financial realities. If you feel safe telling your parents that you need support, they can help you determine what is possible within your resources and budget.

If insurance or government support is not an option and/or you're not in a position to get help from your parents, connect with your school counselor—most of them have access to lists of places to get sliding-scale or subsidized care. Some universities have training programs that provide low-cost support. It is especially important if you're under eighteen to talk very clearly with any counselor about funding and care options, as well as their terms and guidelines for confidentiality and parental consent. Parental-notification and consent laws vary depending on where you are, so before you reveal anything to a therapist, ask them what they are required to report to your parents and/or any authorities, and what they will report anyway. You'll also need to consider your location and how you're going to get to and from your sessions. I once met a therapist that I really loved, but her office was really far from

where I worked, and she didn't accept after-hours appointments. Traveling to my sessions on time was adding stress to my life, so I switched to someone closer. Healing and therapy specifically should be a healthy, supportive experience, not one that causes more strife in your life.

WORDS ABOUT WELLNESS

- The global wellness economy was a $4.5 trillion market in 2018. Weight loss and "healthy eating" initiatives composed more than $700 billion of that sector. — Global Wellness Institute

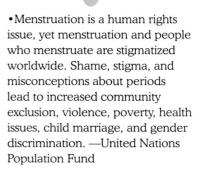

- Menstruation is a human rights issue, yet menstruation and people who menstruate are stigmatized worldwide. Shame, stigma, and misconceptions about periods lead to increased community exclusion, violence, poverty, health issues, child marriage, and gender discrimination. —United Nations Population Fund

- Women who experience autoimmune illnesses including fibromyalgia, depression, endometriosis, and other chronic illnesses are impacted at higher rates than cis men. Women's physical conditions are often dismissed as having a psychological basis versus a physiological origin. —*Prevention Magazine*

• Transgender people experience many health disparities as well as stigma, discrimination, and lack of access to quality care including gender-expansive bathrooms, offering a space on forms and more gender options for transgender and non-binary people to select, and using gender-expansive language when asking about a partner's sexual and relationship history. —American Medical Student Association

• Up to 20% of women attending primary health care facilities in developing countries suffer from anxiety and/or depressive disorders. In most of these centers, patients are not treated. —World Health Organization

• Approximately 80% of 50 million people affected by violent conflicts, civil wars, disasters, and displacement are women and children. At least one in five women experience rape in their lifetime. Each of these factors impacts people's health and wellness. —WHO

• Women, especially women who are overweight, are often not believed and their problems played down. Especially if they are overweight, their health issues are usually attributed to their weight. Weight discrimination in health care has increased by 66% since 1995, especially among women.—*AMA Journal of Ethics*

CALL TO ACTION

• *What is your definition of wellness? How did you come to form this idea? Draw a time line of your thoughts about wellness over time since you were five years old. What have you learned?*

• *The concept of corporate wellness is expensive in our culture. How do you think this relates to colonialism? Racism? Sexism? Caste? Economic status?*

• *How do you want to understand and embody wellness in ten years?*

• *What is one step you can take to care for yourself today, this week, and this month that costs nothing?*

• *What does community care mean to you? What can you foster to make community care more abundant?*

"Males cannot love themselves in patriarchal culture if their very self-definition relies on submission to patriarchal rules. When men embrace feminist thinking and practice, which emphasizes the value of mutual growth and self-actualization in all relationships, their emotional well-being will be enhanced. A genuine feminist politics always brings us from bondage to freedom, from lovelessness to loving." —bell hooks, author, professor, feminist, and social activist

"The notion that women shouldn't care about personal success—or the work that gets them there —is disingenuous; it is impossible for women not to have jobs anymore, so it doesn't make sense to expect them to structure their lives around getting married. The real failure is our cultural incapacity to make room for women to live and thrive outside of traditional conceptions of femininity and relationships. After all, we can eat without marriage, but not without work." —Samhita Mukhopadhyay, writer, editor, and speaker

"Abandon the cultural myth that all female friendships must be bitchy, toxic, or competitive. This myth is like heels and purses—pretty but designed to SLOW women down." — Roxane Gay, author and scholar

CHAPTER TWELVE

Relationships

"Do not become the ones who hurt you. Stay tender with your power." —Chanel Miller, writer and artist

"You've got to learn to leave the table when love's no longer being served." —Nina Simone

A PERSONAL HAIR-STORY: THE TIES THAT (SOMETIMES) BIND US...AND HOPEFULLY LATER TEACH US

When I sat down to think about my longest relationships and how I formed my perspective about them, which then changed over time, I gravitated toward my family unit first.

I was raised in a family structure composed of two cis heterosexual parents and a child, which was celebrated as a cultural ideal in the United States and in many places around the world. I grew up in what was commonly referred to as the **"nuclear family"** throughout the first fifty years of the 20th century. Still, forty years ago, my mom often endured snide and judgmental remarks from other parents at school about her frequent travel schedule for work.

To add to the cringeworthiness of their comments, some folks asked why we had a different last name, with hers being hyphenated with her birth name as a point of personal choice. Years later, I decided to embrace her decision to keep her name by deciding to decline my partner's name completely once I read that women historically took cis men's names as a marker of property ownership. I simply couldn't bear the thought of paying to change my name when I already had publications and a whole life before we met, which he had no role in shaping.

Although my childhood family model fit into what was considered as the ideal basic family unit, I knew that it didn't look like most of the families I actually knew. It also weirded me out that teachers, and sometimes strangers, would praise my father for staying with my family— as if it were somehow unexpected for a Black father to be present and active in our lives.

My father, as the child of a single mother with eight children, grew up in a different family formation. I used to wonder why working-class laboring mothers like my grandmother were regarded as abnormal, unhealthy, or amoral in popular discourse. Although the family she formed didn't look like the structures uplifted on my favorite sitcoms, her home was always full of love and laughter.

At the time, I wasn't aware of the widespread and long-lasting impact of the racist yet influential Moynihan Report (1965) that blamed the roots and persistence of Black poverty in the United States on families helmed by single mothers as a hindrance to social, cultural, economic, and political progress. Today, the lingering and looming presence of this kind of talk remains present in the messages of some right-wing campaign platforms and news networks that stigmatize families that don't fit into a traditionally accepted, specific, heteronormative, two-parent-and-children narrative. Since so many of the media messages I absorbed about Black family structures and specifically about Black motherhood were warped versions of the reality I experienced, I observed for myself what I understood to be the key ingredients for healthy relationships: respect, reciprocity, trust, communication, empathy, consent, and truth-telling. Relationships, just like anything in life, don't have to be perfect or come in a specific form. But they do need to be driven by shared power and consent in order to be equitable, liberating, and healthy for everyone in them, whether they are **monogamous**, **polyamorous**, sexual, **asexual**, or anything in between. Those key values were all things I learned to strengthen, cultivate, and insist upon—not only from other people but most of all within my relationship to myself and others.

> **Relationships don't have to be perfect or come in a specific form. But they do need to be driven by shared power and consent in order to be equitable, liberating, and healthy for everyone in them, whether they are monogamous, polyamorous, sexual, asexual, or anything in between.**

Many years ago, I discovered that one of my longest and most complicated relationships is between myself and my hair. Yes, my hair. When I wrote about my experience over a decade ago in *Rookie Magazine*, I realized that what I called "a personal hair-story" was really a time line of experience I had learning about how to have healthy relationships with myself and others—and how to set boundaries with friends, strangers, frenemies, family, and partners whose behavior and toxic conditioning (pun intended) hurt more than it healed and harmed more than it helped.

For decades, I was "all locked up" in a series of patterns I wasn't ready to face yet. As I began to learn about feminism, I became more aware of my relationship with power, my proximity to privilege, and how much I was influenced by societal pressure to conform to impossible and destructive beauty standards meant to uphold and celebrate a limited version of white, blond, thin, and affluent beauty as a means to gain social "worthiness."

I'd like to claim that I've been able to step away from toxic relationships or belittling situations...but it is simply untrue. For too long, I thought I was the problem to be fixed because I didn't fit in, which made me feel somehow less worthy of love, support, or compassion without proving myself or literally changing myself in order to achieve acceptance. Far from woke, I didn't just wake up one day and see things the way I do today.

It started years ago when I was riding the metro in my former city, Washington, D.C. I'll never forget how I felt when I locked eyes with a teenage couple sitting across from me. I smiled at them and turned on my iPod. A few minutes later, I sensed that they were talking about me. Through the strains of Nina Simone, I heard this high school girl with cocoa-colored skin and chemically straightened hair tell her partner that she wanted dreadlocks like mine. In response, her boyfriend shot her a sharp look, rolled his eyes, and snapped, "Really? Dreads are horrible, dirty, and ugly—especially on girls. You've got 'good hair.' If you want to stay with me, stay pretty and keep your hair straight." Giggling anxiously, the girl glanced at my iPod to confirm that I wasn't listening to their conversation before reassuring him, "I was just kidding. I'll keep my hair nice." I turned up the volume and took some deep breaths to calm my anger. Did they realize how hateful they sounded? As they walked off the train hand in hand, I fought the strong urge to scream, "Don't date him, girl!"

I wish I could say this was the first time I'd overheard that kind of conversation, but it was not. I've been hearing variations on it my whole life. As a southern-born African American girl who attended predominantly white boarding schools, I am well acquainted with the sexism, racism, and colorism that shape people's attitudes toward Black hair. Strangers, friends, family, and ex-loves have tried to make me feel bad about my hair throughout my life. For a long time, it worked. But then one day, I decided that I was done attaching my self-esteem to what other people think I should look like. In my most painful moments, I play back the video of my own memories and wish I had stood up for myself, or refused to absorb toxic behavior as any indicator of my worth or value. But I'd be lying if I didn't tell you that I, like many of us, absorbed limiting narratives from media and some of the candy-colored dreamy teen magazines I read. Although I spoke about strong values and speaking truth to power, there was a strong part of me that screamed out to belong in order to be loved.

'No person is your friend who demands your silence, or denies your right to grow' — Alice Walker

Although it has often been painful, the struggle to love my hair made me who I am today, and I'm grateful for that. It also taught me how to evaluate my relationship with others and myself. Before I learned what Alice Walker wisely taught us, "No person is your friend who demands your silence, or denies your right to grow," I strived too much to be included instead of embracing my difference and my authentic self as my whole and total truth, exclusive of other people's visions or delusions about who they needed me to be to uphold their own narrow story about life, the world, power, gender, sexuality, or race.

Here's how it went:

When I was born, I had so little hair that my parents put a pink headband on my head so that people would know I was a girl. 'Thank the lord she has hair now,' my grandmother said, 'she was a bald little something. We were worried her hair would never grow.'

I asked my mom why my hair didn't bounce around in pigtails. My mom told me that while my hair didn't swing, it could do lots of things, and I should

1980

1985

1984
My family Christmas card featured a picture of me wearing tap shoes, my sequined dance costume, a toothy grin, and a huge sandy-colored Afro. I remember when my parents took the picture. When I think of it now, I realize it was one of the last moments in my life when I felt totally confident and free, blissfully ignorant of mainstream beauty ideals or other people's issues with my hair.

1987
We moved away from our mostly African American community in South Carolina, and I started grade school at a mostly white international school. After growing tired of being called "Medusa" because the ends of my cornrows were braided and decorated with the colorful beads that I loved, I finally begged my mom to fix my hair into a single French braid.

be proud of that. I ignored her, and spent my days running around the house with a towel on my head, pretending that my short little Afro had been transformed into long, flowing locks. My mom told me not to break my neck tossing my 'hair' like the white girls on TV and carefully monitored the ratio of my white Barbies to the black, Asian, and Latina dolls in my collection.

My parents had cultivated their own Afros since the '70s and were especially sensitive about shielding me from media messages that reinforced a white beauty ideal. When they recognized that I was absorbing negative perceptions of my own hair, I received a birthday cake decorated with Rainbow Brite (a white cartoon doll) – with brown skin. They also gave me a copy of Camille Yarbrough's book *Cornrows* to encourage me to be proud of my heritage. I loved the book because it reminded me of my original style icon, my mother, who wore beautiful braided styles and then unraveled them to reveal gorgeous waves that I adored.

■
1988

During gym, we lined up to learn square dancing. I was paired with a gangly blond boy from New Zealand who said he wanted a new partner, and not one with "cotton-candy hair." My cheeks burned as my classmates laughed. The teacher responded by silently walking me away from the boy and placing me with another girl as a dance partner instead. Later that afternoon, I snuck into the bathroom so I could squeeze my Afro puffs in my hand. Did they really feel like cotton candy? My hair felt so wonderfully springy in my hands—why would that be a bad thing? A few days later, I asked my mom if I could get a "baby relaxer" from a kiddie-perm line, *Just for Me*. My mom said I was too young and would have to wait. I honestly liked my hair because it was soft and reminded me of my dad's Afro, but I was tired of being singled out at school. I pestered my parents to let me relax it because I wanted to look like the other girls.

During a family reunion, I heard one of my older cousins whisper to my straight-haired, tan-skinned multiracial grandmother, "It's a good thing Jamia is a good talker and she's smart, because she sure doesn't look like much compared with her cousins." I looked around at my family, saw the ones with lighter skin and silky hair, and contrasted it with my darker shade and kinky head. My face grew hot with anger, but I refused to give her the satisfaction. I thought to myself, "I'll always be smart" and resolved to take that on as my shield. Still, it got to me. A few months later, I convinced my mom to let me get my hair straightened. The chemical relaxer burned my scalp and my curls. Thirty minutes later, I finally had hair that swung when I shook my head. But it wasn't long before I came to resent how it would frizz up, and how the maintenance required for me to get in the pool prevented me from joining the swim team. I decided to get hair extensions. All that fuss made me wish I had the courage to wear it in dreadlocks like my style icon, Lisa Bonet.

1990

1995

Our family hairdresser, Betty, told me that I had pretty eyes like Lisa "Left Eye" Lopes (RIP) and commanded me to ask my mom if I could stop getting braided extensions and get my hair relaxed instead. Betty gave me bangs to match Left Eye's and showed me how to blow-dry my hair straight and wrap it at night. She instructed me to get $60 touch-ups every few weeks so no "nappy hairs" would ruin my look. While I had reservations about the cost and time investment required, I took her advice and basked in the compliments, even when they came in the form of underhanded comments about my natural look. I'll never forget how, on one of my first dates, the guy looked at me and said, "Wow, with your hair straight like that you are almost beautiful." I grimaced and turned my face away as he tried to kiss me. I wondered what he thought of his own cropped kinky coils.

When I was seventeen, I saved money from my internships and summer job and took a trip to the city to get a "Hawaiian Silky" human-hair weave. My boarding school roommates named the weave "Baywatch Barbie," as if it had an identity of its own. I noticed that the attention I received from #basic cis het boys skyrocketed. It made me feel ill that the weave made such a difference. Did these boys like me or my fake hair? I waited too long to take the weave out—I wanted to get the most for my money!—and when I did, it had become matted to my head. Getting it off required me to rip out clumps of my real hair and made my scalp irritated. I began considering putting an end to my war with my natural hair.

1997

1998

I started my freshman year of college with a fresh new head of braid extensions. Even though I thought I had learned my lesson with the weave debacle of 1997, I was afraid to wear my hair free when starting college. After so many years of hiding it, I felt vulnerable wearing it natural and guilty for not being able to stomach the prospect of being marginalized or judged for the way I looked. As part of my course, I was assigned a research project on censorship in schools. I read up on the media controversy surrounding Carolivia Herron's *Nappy Hair*, a children's book that destigmatizes and celebrates natural hair. Even though I spent my time in school passionately arguing that Herron's book be taught in schools despite parental objection, I still wasn't brave enough to bare (or bear!) my own hair. I spent half of the money I earned on extensions that took hours to braid into my curls, to make sure I looked "presentable."

An elderly professor pulled me aside and told me that I could have a long career in broadcast journalism because I was "articulate" and have a "young face that will ensure a longer shelf life as a female reporter." But he also warned me that I could never work with my hair in braids and told me to think about changing my hairstyle to fit in more with more "professional" looks worn by other Black women on TV. I didn't want to choose between my job and my hair, so I switched my major to print and then finally to public relations. I regret how much I took that professor's words to heart, but I am also grateful for them. That interaction gave me a push to begin pursuing my passion, feminist media activism.

1998

1999

I went to see feminist royalty bell hooks read at Vertigo Books for the launch of her children's book *Happy to Be Nappy*, a beautiful story about brown girls celebrating their natural hair texture. I was delighted to see kids of all colors using positive words to describe "nappy" hair. I then discovered an online community for natural hair. For five years, I longed to try dreadlocks, but my fear of being judged held me back—so every few months, I forked over almost as much money as my rent to get my hair done. In the meantime, I pasted pictures of Lisa Bonet and Lauryn Hill into my journal to inspire myself to do what I knew in my heart I needed to do—stop hiding my real hair.

After I broke up with a boyfriend (who told me that I couldn't pull off short hair or dreads), I cut all my hair off. I washed that dude out of my hair, and years of self-loathing and racist conditioning went down the drain too. I went around town holding my Afro'd head high, loving the feeling of the air on my neck and the lightness of not having fake hair on my head. As my hair grew longer, I did what I'd been longing to do for years and started twisting it into dreads. I wondered what took me so long. My hair was healthier than ever, but others still asked whether my hair was clean, real, or fake. My grandma, always the head member of the hair police, asked me if she could pay me $50 to press and iron my hair back to "nice and normal." While she denied her tendency to sometimes promote colorism or the existence of her own light-skinned privilege, she said things like, "Well you did end up dark like your Mom but at least you ended up with semi-good hair and smaller features like mine. Why would you make it look more nappy if you could easily press it to make it straight?"

2004

2005

While riding the metro in DC, I felt a strange tug. I whipped around to see a white man in a business suit standing behind me with a smug look on his face. "I've always wanted to touch that kind of hair and wondered what it felt like," he said, oblivious to my disgust. A few months later, I was flirting with the gorgeous, shaved-head son of a family friend when he asked, "Do you always wear your hair in braids or locs? Do you think you will ever change it? You're so pretty, so I was just wondering if it will always be like that—you could be even prettier." I responded by rolling my eyes, laughing, and sniping: "People with no hair shouldn't tell people with hair how to wear it." I realized then that my new style was a great litmus test for evaluating dating prospects. If a guy was going to try to change my hair, he was probably going to try to control me in other ways. If he was superficial enough to tell me how to style my hair, he was probably lacking the depth I was looking for in a partner.

I was racing to a graduate school class at NYU when a man began his catcalls. When I ignored him, he began serenading me: "You dirty-dreads b**ch, oh dirty dreads." I ignored him in the moment but went back to my apartment, raging inside. I went over all of the things I wished that I'd yelled at him, and then felt guilty about giving a random street harasser so much of my precious time and energy. A few weeks later, the radio host Don Imus called Rutgers University's mostly Black women's basketball team "nappy-headed hos," and I once again felt the weight of the culture of racist misogyny that fills our streets and our airwaves.

2007
∎

I LOVE MY CURLS

A friend's five-year-old son looked at me with big blue eyes and asked, "Mia why do you wear your hair so crazy?" I pointed to his wavy blond hair and said, "Well, why do you wear your hair so crazy? I love my hair." He smiled and said, "I love your hair also." I told him that I love his curls, too.

2011
∎

2010
∎

When I heard *Sesame Street*'s natural-haired brown Muppet girl sing "I Love My Hair," I wished that I'd had such a tune to hum when I was a child. Joey Mazzarino, the head writer of Sesame Street, told NPR that he produced the segment because his adopted Ethiopian daughter "wanted to have long blond hair and straight hair, and she wanted to be able to bounce it around." It made me sad to see how little had changed for African American girls since my days running around with the towel on my head, and grateful that this man, for one, was encouraging his daughter to love her natural hair.

BE PROUD OF YOUR HAIR

2012

Even though having dreadlocks seems more mainstream now—I see more people than ever before wearing them on the streets and on TV—I still get tons of questions about my hair from young women of color who are contemplating going natural. I am still frequently asked the following questions:

EMBRACE YOUR HAIR

Q: So…how long have you had your locs?
A: Eight years.
Q: Is it all yours?
A: Yes.
Q: Can you wash your hair?
A: Yes.
Q: It looks really clean. Are you sure it isn't braids?
A: Yes. It is really "clean," and it is not braids.
Q: Can I feel it?
A. Maybe, if I like you. No, if I don't.
Q: What does it feel like?
A: Hair.
Q: Does it hurt? (Often said while tugging at one of my locs without asking.)
A: No. But yes, if you pull it hard like you just did.
Q: Have you ever had difficulty finding a job because of it?
A: No, not that I know of.

While I still get these questions pretty frequently, I am less bothered these days by how other people respond to my hair While the world hasn't changed that much since I started dealing with my own internalized racism, I have shifted my attitude to embrace my hair rather than resist it.

It's still a challenging choice to make, but nowadays, there are many supportive and dynamic online spaces for women transitioning to and maintaining natural hair. I keep visiting these sites to hear about other women's experiences with going natural, because their stories give me hope that we are (slowly but surely) getting better at accepting beauty in all its forms.

The days when my hair defined me are over, but my 'do still reminds me of the changes I've made, the growth and the pain. My awesome dreads represent my hard-won liberation from expectations, judgment, self-hate, racist and sexist conditioning. For that, I am grateful to my hair. Today, as writer (and my former editor at *Rookie*) Danielle Henderson says on her website, I wear it natural "on purpose." Why? Because my locs are a constant reminder of where I've been and where I've grown within my relationship with myself and my relationships with others. My hair journey taught me about self and community love for my heritage, boundaries, consent, self-actualization, and (sometimes painfully and other times lovingly) how to let go of people who couldn't understand my growth.

I chose to focus on my relationship with my hair because I figured out how much something as seemingly simple as my tresses impacted how I related to people in my family, at work, romantically, and so forth. For me, hair was all about my relationship to power, and it took years to figure out that I had the right to determine how I chose to engage with others instead of just accepting how they chose to project their expectations on to me.

My hair-story started as a rebellion to prove to others that I didn't need to fit their standards to love myself. Over time, I began to see that the key relationship I needed to heal, prioritize, and nuture was my own in order to reflect the same dignity, respect, compassion, and acceptance onto others.

CALL TO ACTION

•*What have you learned about relationships throughout your life? What role does power play in your relationships? At home, at school, and at work?*

•*Does feminism inform how you form your relationships?*

•*Did the family you grew up in shape how you think about relationships? Why or why not?*

•*Did my experiences with harassment, colorism, or shaming resonate with you? Have you experienced anything similar? What might you do or say to disrupt this dynamic the next time it happens?*

•*What is one step you can take this week to address an unbalanced or unjust power dynamic in your relationships? Is there a boundary you can set? A need you would like to see met? A desire you'd like to share? Take some time to write down what comes up for you and think about what it would feel like to ask for these changes from the other parties you're involved with.*

LEGENDARY LEADERS BY 25

69 BC—Cleopatra, last ruler of the
Ptolemaic Kingdom of Egypt

1412—Joan of Arc, French
heroine and saint

1945—Sarah Weddington, attorney
who won the *Roe v. Wade* case legalizing
reproductive freedom in the United States.

1995—Weng Yu Ching,
LGBTQIA+ rights activist

1999—Emma Gonzalez,
activist and gun control
advocate

2003—Isra Hirsi,
environmental activist

1759—Mary Wollstonecraft, writer, editor, feminist advocate

1930—Lorraine Hansberry, playwright and writer

1996—Tavi Gevinson, writer, editor, actress

1997—Malala Yousafzai, Nobel Laureate

2003—Greta Thunberg, environmental activist

2004—Autumn Peltier, water protector

2007—Amariyanna "Mari" Copeny "Little Miss Flint" activist

So accustomed have male media leaders become to the wealth and decision-making power they command they just can't parse the notion of equality between the sexes. They have never understood the world feminists actually envision, in which women and men share equal educational, economic, and professional opportunities, live free of abuse, can be fully sexual without judgment or coercion, and where people can embrace their authentic selves." —Jennifer Pozner, media critic and author

"Most of us believe knowledge is power, but only power is power. Power comes from owning our media outlets and owning our stories. That's why I'm out here fighting for Net Neutrality — the power to control our own voice on the internet." —Malkia Cyril, media justice activist and poet

"The more I read about this 'beauty myth' and intense scrutiny over women's appearance, the more I started noticing that women in my life, across generations, were affected by the pressure to be beautiful and consume."
—Elena Rossini, filmmaker

CHAPTER FOURTEEN

Media

"The women of color like Carol Jenkins who entered mainstream newsrooms in the 1970s have done us an enormous favor. Because of them we have had great reporters emerge in the last decade, like Rachel Swarns at the New York Times, who broke the story that Georgetown University sold enslaved people to sustain the survival of the institution."
—Rinku Sen, writer, political strategist, and former publisher

MEDIA: WHAT'S YOUR LENS?

Some people refer to the media, the most potent public education tool in our lives, as the "eyes of the world." As someone who is **monocular** and was born partially blind, I often think of this metaphor in the context of my own life as a media activist, media maker, and human seeing the world in my specific way, with one lens-less (true story) eye open.

When I was born, my great-grandma said I had "hungry eyes"—the same kind of sparkly peepers she saw in babies destined to become quick, smart, and self-possessed adults. My kinfolks say she told everyone to get ready because I was going to be "a firecracker." She looked at my eyes and saw my soul before I knew myself. And luckily, I grew up with that story so that I could focus on it—instead of the other one I heard too often about how my eyes were somehow less than because I was born with "a lazy eye" with a freckle on it, a congenital cataract, and a malformed optic nerve.

Great-grandma was right. Regardless of my visual limitations—and in many cases because of them—I can see my life and the world I'm a part of, more clearly than ever. But if I relied on the media and how others responded to me based on my physical inability to look like what they were conditioned to see "as normal" or "healthy," I would never know that nothing about me was broken or needed to be "fixed." I wish I learned early on that the injustices of systems that don't work for all of us are the problem, not us for not fitting into their confines.

When I receive unsolicited sexist comments from cis men about how much prettier I'd look if I switched from glasses to contacts *on air* when I go on camera for a TV appearance, or recommendations for ophthalmologists who can help "straighten out" my eye to make it less "distracting," I remember that these same eyes are the ones my great-grandma saw aflame with the fire of curiosity and audacity.

I share my story and own it because girls, young people, people with disabilities, queer, LGBTQIA+, and BIPOC folks are often force-fed stories that present a stunted definition of who we are. I know firsthand that amplifying our voices in the media and bringing them from the margins to the center is a way to make the various communities we represent visible, as well as to make sure our recollection of history is more inclusive.

All too often, we receive cultural, social, and political messages that tell us that our value is based on our ability to fit into a narrow ideal rather than our ability to lead, teach, transform, and enact change. One of the reasons I love to read about past generations is to look back on folks who were bold and brave enough to express themselves despite grave obstacles. When I think of the folks who relied on their innate sense of knowing, I am reminded to cherish my entire self and my voice, to protect and defend it with sacred ferocity, and to "love it hard" no matter who tells me that I am not "enough" in a world rife with misogyny, ableism, sizeism, racism, homophobia, and transphobia.

Like everyone else, mine is a long story with twists and turns of fragmentation and contradiction because, like Baby Suggs said in one of my favorite books, *Beloved*, many of the messages I continue to receive still apply, and, yes, more often than I'd like it feels like "yonder they do not love this flesh" or this voice. They—the online bullies, the media, the

fashion industrial complex, and advertisers sometimes "despise my voice and my flesh" as they try to invade my mind every day to make me feel like who I am is disposable, replaceable, and less than, but I write anyway, and I speak regardless—because I genuinely believe that **if we don't define ourselves someone else will.**

In a media where only 3% of clout positions are female, where Wikipedia is mostly edited by cis college-educated men, and people of color are vastly under-represented, I feel called to record and honor the truth and to unearth experiences that might otherwise be ignored, stigmatized, or left in a shroud of silence. Throughout my life, I have seen how media specifically impacts how we perceive ourselves and our bodies. I remember growing up

and having my parents sit me down at dinner to "deprogram" me when I wanted to straighten my hair so I could have a side ponytail like the silken-haired white actors on T.V. instead of an Afro puff. I wondered why in Saudi Arabia, where I grew up, I could see that one of America's biggest exports was a toxic body culture when I heard my friends in the neighborhood were dieting to look like mostly white US and European TV stars, bleaching their skin with creams, dyeing their hair platinum blond with Sun-In, and asking traveling pals to bring them back diet pills on summer vacations back in the United States.

Remember when I went to college and decided to switch my concentration to public relations instead of broadcast journalism? I did that in part because I was terrified by a message I heard from an old white male media professor who said I would have to straighten my hair in order to be taken seriously in the media.

Essentially, I was being told that I would need to change my authentic self to be on camera because my voice would not matter in the natural body it was in. I now know that I shouldn't have listened to his naysaying, but when this interaction happened, I understood that the media shapes our understanding of who we are and what we can be. And that was a lesson that helped

drive me toward the work I am passionate about today as a feminist media activist and professional storyteller.

We live in a reality where there is a shortage of stories by and for women in the media, where we are only seen, heard, or read about in mainstream broadcast and print media 24% of the time. The trouble is that women in the media are "treated like ornaments and not instruments," as my friend feminist author and organizer, Gloria Steinem says. As a result, we, especially BIPOC, disabled folks, and LGBTQIA+ people, are most likely to be supporting characters rather than the lead.

When our voices are missing, the brilliance and wisdom of over half of the population are wasted.

We're missing most of the story when we perpetuate tired, outdated stereotypes about so-called ice princesses, bad girls, catfights and the like. We cannot have "fair and balanced" media coverage when people from marginalized genders are not represented equally at the tables that decide what is funded, published, broadcast, or publicized.

In addition to representation, we require full participation in the cultural institutions that impact our lives.

TAKING CONTROL OF THE NARRATIVE: A CASE STUDY ON QUEEN BEY

You didn't think I could talk about media without writing about Beyoncé, did you? For the millennial generation, Beyoncé is to innovation what Madonna was to reinvention for Generation X. Beyoncé is representative of a generation that has been progressively forced into a **"freelance economy,"** who embrace social entrepreneurship and innovation. Beyoncé's groundbreaking self-titled surprise release of her 2013 visual album (without promotion) aligned with a cultural shift towards proactive, creative, and collaborative social enterprise.

Beyoncé illuminates the distinction between the "selfie" generation's mischaracterization of selfishness and the motives of **self-actualization**. She does this by fearlessly asserting her feminist allegiances and deploying her privilege, access, and platform to bring greater awareness and nuance to the ways people perceive feminism and feminists in mainstream culture.

Although Beyoncé has long been associated with feminism by the time of the publication of this book, it wasn't always the case. While some critics say that Beyoncé is perpetuating oppressive systems that undermine rather than empower, I consider her unapologetic embrace of self-actualization, bodily autonomy, and expressions of solidarity in line with the very values that inspire many younger women.

Perhaps some of the backlash stems from some folks not being used to seeing Black and Brown bodies wielding that sort of privilege and power in the mainstream? Beyoncé disrupts the notion that women performers must always sacrifice their agency and creative license to the wills of a mostly cis-white male-dominated corporate music industry. She disturbs conventional discourse about women's rights in the public square by unapologetically embracing her contradictions.

After a decade of hearing older feminists ask, "Where are the young women?" and reading trite pieces about feminism's inevitable demise (again!) in the media, it's refreshing to see Beyoncé inspire a focus on young women and feminism in the public sphere. In the aftermath of her album's success, it's no surprise that Beyoncé's leadership inspired a bandwagon of feminist proclamations from celebrities, including J. Lo, Katy Perry, and Miley Cyrus—and a string of others who followed suit. While commodifying and rebranding feminism is not the path to true liberation, it does beg the question: are we getting closer to a cultural tipping point after the rise of the #MeToo Movement, Black Lives Matter, and the Women's March?

Instead of asking for permission from established feminist institutions, academics, and industry stakeholders, Beyoncé harnessed the power of the interwebs to virally share her artistic feminist intervention and influence the cultural conversation.

With magazine cover stories like *The Nation's* controversial piece about so-called "feminist twitter wars," it could be argued that rather than adopting a new icon, the feminist movement needs more cohesiveness, inclusion, and collaboration—this is precisely why Beyoncé is a useful messenger for the next generation of advocates.

Without claiming to have all of the answers or to possess the end-all, be-all solutions to critical issues that are affecting women's lives

every day, her visual and lyrical insistence on defining herself as a feminist and her assertion of strength as a woman, breadwinner, mother, partner, and sexual being will make feminism accessible to women and girls who were previously alienated.

By using her megaphone to advance her intersectional vision for equality on her own terms, Beyoncé sends young women a valuable message—you are the CEO of your own life. Don't "lean in" to someone else's industry or institution, create and then define your own.

To be sure, some radical feminists will see this as a celebration of **"choice feminism."** Others may share my view that the complexities of Beyoncé's public exploration of her own identity via her evolving discography—from *Beyoncé* to *Lemonade*, to "Apesh*t," to "Savage"—philanthropy, and activism, show that as she begins to control more of the media herself, she has more ownership of her message.

SMELLS LIKE MEDIA SEXISM: REFLECTIONS MEDIA, ELECTIONS, AND GENDER

During the fall prior to the 2016 US Presidential election, I wrote an op-ed for *New York Times'* Room for Debate series that asked participants whether Hillary Clinton's feminism was out of style. While I shared my frustration with my editor about the nature of the question (since I doubted whether Donald Trump would be asked if his discordant brand of winner-takes-all bullying was out of style), I contributed my thoughts to the debate.

In my piece, I argued that for young gender justice advocates, the movement for equality must be multi-issue, adaptable, and inclusive. I quoted feminist writer Audre Lorde's wisdom that **"there is no such thing as a single-issue struggle because we do not live single-issue lives."** I mentioned that I recognized a shift in messaging from Hillary Clinton since her run in 2008, which seemed to be evolving along with the culture change.

Clinton's historic popular vote victory—but ultimately ill-fated presidential run—emerged during the height of #feministactivism. Although Lorde imparted her words about us not living single-issue lives more than twenty years ago, the future of the movement for gender equality is still being fueled by her foresight. Hillary Clinton even included a line that was likely influenced by intersectional activism on the internet. In her "Breaking Barriers" speech to Black voters at the Schomburg Center in New York City, Clinton said, "we're not a single-issue country," signifying her journeyed but eventual embrace of

HILLARY CLINTON

THERE IS NO SUCH THING AS A SINGLE-ISSUE STRUGGLE

the reality that candidates seeking support from diverse next-generation feminists must, advance an agenda that acknowledges the connection between race, class, gender, disability, and economic justice.

From viral hashtag campaigns like #YesAllWomen, a reaction to misogynist murders and gendered gun violence at the University of California, Santa Barbara, to the campaign to #FreeKesha from being forced to work with the Sony producer she says sexually abused her, to spirited public debates about the limitations of best-selling book *Lean In*'s self-empowerment message in the face of stifling systemic barriers for BIPOC women, trans, and nonbinary folks, online feminist activism contributed to shaping public discourse, influenced the US presidential election, and paved the way for future action on the ground.

Unsurprisingly, the virality of these online campaigns and the boon of feminist messaging in pop culture by celebrities also influenced the broader discourse. But their escalated awareness and engagement owes itself in many ways to the outreach and activism of intersectional activists who used online media to democratize their access to people whose platforms could spread their advocacy far and wide. For example, in *Lenny* magazine—a now nonoperational online feminist newsletter with interviews with Hillary Clinton, and Senator Kirsten Gillibrand—Emma Watson connected with celebrated feminist scholar bell hooks. Watson publicly announced that she would be taking a year off to study feminism. *Orange is the New Black*'s Matt McGorry, partnered with a feminist firm to launch a digital campaign to support and fundraise for reproductive rights.

KIRSTEN GILLIBRAND

ORANGE IS THE NEW BLACK

Four years later, I reflected on that period of time when I signed on as one of over two hundred Black women who called on presumptive nominee Joe Biden to select a Black woman running mate. When I watched then-Senator Kamala Harris take the stage at the 2020 Democratic Convention on TV, I remembered our letter that read, "We urge you to seize this historic opportunity to choose a Black woman running mate who will fight for the issues that matter most to the American people."

While the words in our memo remain meaningful, the message that stands out to me is that our voices are powerful when we come together and speak our truth. In addition to being proud to see a Black and South Asian woman who was told she was not "likeable enough" or "electable" by media pundits and online naysayers, I was encouraged by the reminder that instead of being idle consumers of media, we can also make and shape media with grassroots advocacy, media campaigns, direct action demonstrations, and even creating our own platforms too.

"We urge you to seize this historic opportunity to choose a Black woman running mate who will fight for the issues that matter most to the American people."

FEMINIST PRESSES ARE FROM THE FUTURE: EVEN IF THEY WERE BORN IN THE PAST.

Book publishing is political, and no matter when and where it happens, the revolution almost surely will be published. But we can't change our culture until we fundamentally transform the literary landscape to center the voices of the **global majority**. That's why intersectional feminist publishing is resistance.

The industry that produces the majority of our books is too often a gated community in need of rapid change. As one of the 5% of Black publishing professionals across the globe, I yearn for an industry that looks more like the diverse sea of faces I see on the subway every day than our current monochromatic reality. Since books help shape our understanding of who we are and what we're capable of in the world, the robust amplification of under-represented voices in editorial and critical decision-making positions is essential to capturing our full human story.

I think back again to when I was told that I would need to change myself to be on camera as a broadcaster and that my voice and words would not matter unless they were packaged in a body that fit into a very narrow standard. I wanted to be a reporter because I watched the news religiously as an expat kid in Saudi Arabia, but rarely saw myself reflected in the anchors. I loved media, but I also wanted to be a role model for girls of color. As a child, I never envisaged having a leadership role in publishing for the same reasons, and it has inspired me to consider what we can do to disrupt gatekeeping and open doors for more diversity in the industry at all levels, from writers to editors, to designers and reviewers.

Influenced by my parents who fought for my freedom as **civil rights organizers** and by the gender segregation I witnessed in Saudi Arabia, I have dedicated myself to fighting for gender and racial justice. I work to bring diverse voices from the margins to the center through thought leadership, media justice activism, and progressive publishing as a feminist publisher and book author.

In 2017, I joined the Feminist Press (F.P.) in its forty-seventh year. At the time, I became the youngest and the first woman of color executive director and publisher of the longest-running feminist publisher in the world. When I received the call about my new role, I felt proud to lead an organization that served as the vanguard of feminist publishing for nearly five decades.

As I set out to expand the Press's long and proven track record of publishing intersectional books, including the first Black feminist studies reader *But Some of Us Are Brave*, Zora Neale Hurston's *I Love Myself When I Am Laughing But Then Again When I Am Looking Mean And Impressive*, and its *Women Writing India* and *Women Writing Africa* series, I pledged to do whatever was in my power to help create systems every day that would help make it possible for future leaders of the press to reflect the diversity of its intersectional and iconic list. A few years later, Roxane Gay put these intentions into words when we spoke together at an event about the opportunities and challenges that come with being the "first." In essence, she said **the important thing to remember about being the first is to make sure that we are not the last.**

Our culture is in the midst of a seismic shift, as women, people of color, nonbinary and transgender people, and other minorities are raising their voices and taking charge like never before. Yet the publishing industry lags far behind. It is ruled by both demographic **homogeneity**—79% white, 88% heterosexual, 99% cisgender, and 92% non-disabled, according to a 2015 survey of North American publishers—while a shift is happening, we have a lot more we can do to uplift writing from marginalized communities.

As an activist press, F.P. set out to realize its dream of creating a more just world where everyone recognizes themselves in a book. F.P. welcomes participation from a broad spectrum of voices as writers, editors, publicists, and designers while producing the essential feminist texts for our time. The work itself revolutionizes publishing by modeling practices of justice and collaboration throughout the organization's operations.

At the same time, I reflected on what social, economic, political, and cultural conditions made it take so long for the leadership of a trailblazing publisher whose diverse and storied list filled both my mother's and my own bookshelf to be helmed by a Black woman. Due to my experiences as one of the few younger women of color in leadership positions in various organizations and companies throughout my life, questions about who is not in the room and who is being left out remain at the forefront of my mind.

Whenever I am contemplating new initiatives, systems, and structures, I think about how to make our work more sustainable and accessible to future leaders that might not have the privileges I do. I wish this were the norm instead of the exception, and that's why I work diligently to live this into existence because I have yearned for it so much throughout my career in online, print, and other media and activist spaces.

"We will raise this wounded world into a wondrous one...There is always light, if only we're brave enough to see it. If only we're brave enough to be it."

—Amanda Gorman, poet

As a movement press of discovery, we tapped into the momentum conjured by the aftermath of the Women's March, the largest recorded march in the history of the world, and other important activist movements that ramped up after the 2016 elections, including labor movements, the fight for reproductive justice, the #MeToo movement, the Kavanaugh hearing protests, the Black Lives Matter uprisings, and the publishing day of solidarity. The Feminist Press publishes the texts our culture needs to move the needle forward: stories that inspire

Like some of the other nonprofits I worked at prior to F.P., although progressive values, diversity, inclusion, and racial justice remained integral to our organization, we grappled with structural barriers inherent to the institutions we worked within, including higher education and making our case to funders in the philanthropic world, in the context of late-stage **capitalism**, patriarchy, and **white supremacy** during the Trump era.

people to listen and learn from one another, to resist injustice in all its forms, and to take action. In our own way, F.P.'s small but mighty team endeavored to change publishing by infusing our own values into practice, bringing new voices into the conversation at all levels of our organization via paid publishing apprenticeships, diverse writing prizes, and accessible events, using storytelling as a powerful tool for social justice and building empathy.

While we advanced feminist publishing by working with feminist typographers, BIPOC, queer, trans, and disabled artists, illustrators, and collaborators and more, we also existed within a landscape where feminism became the word of the year in *Merriam-Webster's Dictionary*, which led some folks to ask us if we still needed to exist despite attacks on free expression and diversity as authoritarianism rose.

Born out of a cultural zeitgeist in 1970, F.P. uses its position as an activist publisher to build spaces, communities, and structures that are more inclusive and transformative. When Florence Howe founded the Feminist Press almost a half-century ago, she anticipated that the need for a feminist publisher would end in a decade or so once the industry caught on to the importance of this work. Although some progress has been made, it is clear we will have our work cut out for us for another fifty to one hundred years or more, until the same root causes that ignited the need for the Feminist Press and other radical presses to exist fifty years ago are addressed with just, equitable, and inclusive solutions.

In the aftermath of several innovative and iconic feminist media publications, including *The Establishment, The Hairpin,* *Lenny Letter, Rookie Magazine, XoJane* shuttering over the past decade due to a turbulent economic landscape, former *Feministing* and current *Teen Vogue* executive editor Samhita Mukhopadhyay spoke about the vital need for narrative power in independent and progressive spaces despite the increase of intersectional feminist conversations within the broader culture. "Many of us involved in the feminist blogosphere are now in mainstream media, and that's exciting. That said, we need independent media because they're an important check," she affirms, uplifting why we—and culture at large—benefit from sites of discovery and **insurgency**. We grow as a result of the emergent thinking that illuminates the path for a broader conversation beyond what mostly money-driven markets and formulas can tell us. Publishing houses like F.P. are "the check." Publications and platforms that breed nuance, celebrate complexity, capture riskier conversations, and lean into questions without surefire answers will always be relevant. By training the next generation of literary changemakers and acting as a springboard for diverse publishing professionals, we must cultivate large-scale change and promote a more equitable, just world for all.

THE STATE OF PUBLISHING: A QUICK HIT ABOUT WHY WE CAN'T TALK ABOUT FEMINISM WITHOUT TALKING ABOUT RACE AND CLASS

If you want to go from a numbers aspect, the publishing industry is primarily made up of women.

OPEN PARTICIPATION IS POWERFUL

In 2015 and 2016, *Publishers Weekly* stated that 74% of the US publishing industry was made up of women.
• 88% of those women were heterosexual
• 79% were white
• Asians/Native Hawaiians/Pacific Islanders made up 7.2% of staff
• Hispanics/Latinos/Mexicans 5.5%
• Black/African Americans 3.5%
In that same year, cis men still made more money.
• In 2015, men in the industry earned an average of $96,000
• In 2015, women earned an average of $61,000
Even with women represented in the industry at executive and board levels, 40% of the respondents were men.

There are over 3.3 billion women living in the world.

Yet if you judge solely by the mainstream media, you might conclude that those 3.3 billion people are less intelligent, less articulate, and have less to say about issues (even those directly affecting them) than cis men. In addition, the absence of their voices reinforces retrograde stereotypes that undermine women, transgender, and nonbinary people's agency, leadership, and power.

According to a study of seventy countries by the World Bank and published in the *American Political Science Review*, grassroots feminist movement-building is more crucial to ending gender-based violence than left-wing political parties, national wealth, or the number of women politicians. Yet, the reality is that women, transgender, and nonbinary people are less likely to own media, drive the public narrative, and have fair and diverse representation and access. What's more, the prevalence of online harassment, abuse, and victim blaming hinders women's ability to freely and safely express their stories and opinions.

That's why I devoted over a decade of my life to participating in or supporting feminist and other progressive media justice movements at organizations like my Women's Media Center; Women in Media and News; Free Press; Fair; the former

Here's an overview of the current media landscape and where we are:

- Sexist media holds women and non-binary folks back from political parity
- Most media aren't aware of the full extent of the double standard
- Press are often more interested in a woman candidate's shoes than her opinions during political elections.
- A media where victim blaming, slut shaming, and implicit bias run rampant.

Here's how we're trying to move:

- To shape the debate and move the needle with intersectional, decentralized, bottom-up, youth-led, consciousness raising, community-driven, accessible, rapid-response, and sustainable solutions and movements

Women, Action, and the Media; Hollaback! Center for Media Justice; Miss Representation, Color of Change; and Ultraviolet. Media justice organizations like these emerged to democratize media ownership, build people power, resources, and influence to ignite a significant power shift that increases women, BIPOC, and gender-nonconforming people's media and tech access, ownership, representation, and participation within the next decade.

Media rights and media justice organizations generate media and tech disruptions and partnerships, research and document disparities in the media, develop plans and strategies to hold media outlets and platforms accountable for barriers to equal access, and expand our personal and community capacity to influence media.

Media accountability campaigns help catalyze infrastructure changes in the media and tech industries by pushing for more intersectional approaches and research data to help inform partnerships and solutions that allow people who are traditionally marginalized in these spaces to freely and safely access free speech, free expression, and online media resources in an inclusive and sustainable way.

Here's where we want to go:

GENDER JUSTICE

INCLUDES AND UPLIFTS VOICES

- A media fueled by gender and racial justice that addresses barriers to access, participation, and ownership.
- A media that promotes a collaborative strategy and vision with shared power and expands the influence and capacity of the people, not just those who make profits.
- A media that includes and uplifts the voices of all, not some.
- A media where media makers and professionals are trained and supported in media literacy and media justice work around trauma-informed reporting, reproductive justice, racial justice, sexual assault, and disabilities.

RACIAL JUSTICE

(ONLINE) SAFETY IN NUMBERS

In 2016, after several years of campaigning against online harassment and abuse in media, I moderated a conversation about women in the media and online harassment with State Senator Wendy Davis, current Miss Representation executive director Soraya Chemaly, and Smart Girls at the Party's Meredith Walker at SXSW's first-ever online harassment summit in March. The *Austin American-Statesman* captured our stories about the impact of online abuse. Soon after, President Obama name-checked the Summit and said **"The internet is a public space where women deserve to live safely and without fear."**

Although more is known about the impact and prevalence of online harassment today, its disturbing and sometimes deadly impact persists. Here's a snapshot:

• Currently, 90% of United States journalists and 71% in Canada noted online harassment as the largest threat facing journalists. Fifty percent of these journalists said they experienced online threats. Only a small portion of this group reported that they received digital safety training in their workplace. — Committee to Protect Journalists

• Forty-one percent of women who experienced online abuse reported that they had at least one experience where online harassment threatened their feeling of physical safety. Worldwide, 46% of women surveyed said that the digital abuse and harassment they experienced was misogynistic or sexist. —Amnesty International

• In the United States, 40% of people have experienced online abuse, and more than 60% have witnessed it. BIPOC and LGBTQIA+ people are disproportionately targeted, and women are twice as likely as men to experience sexual harassment and abuse online. — Pew Research

- Two-thirds of women journalists have been harassed, with more than half experiencing online abuse within the past year. —International Women's Media Foundation and Troll Busters

- Almost a quarter of women surveyed in eight countries experienced online abuse or harassment at least once, including 16% of surveyed respondents in Italy and 33% in the U.S.—Amnesty International

CALL TO ACTION

- *What impact has media had in your life? Take a moment to jot down a list of the types of media you consume during the course of three days. What messages do you receive about who you are? What messages are you picking up about other people whose identities or backgrounds are different from your own? Who has power in the media you consume? Who is left out?*

- *What are some ways we can examine culture to reshape how we understand and perceive systems like the current media we have?*

- *Imagine yourself as a producer of media. Sketch a quick outline of the media you'd like to see in the world that has yet to exist. What conditions would need to be present for this kind of storytelling to thrive?*

- *Have you ever experienced online harassment or abuse? How did it make you feel? How did it impact your relationship to power? If it happens again, know you are not alone. Organizations like Crisis Text Line, Women's Media Center, GLAAD, Hollaback!'s HeartMob, PEN, and others have resources to help you get the help you need as you assess your safety, document the abuse, and determine whether to block, mute, report, use counter speech, or take further action with the support of trusted allies in your life.*

- *How does social power impact the difference between equal representation in the media and justice in the media for all people? What role does privilege play in who is seen, heard, represented, and given ownership of media outlets, platforms, and systems in your community, country, or culture?*

"Activism is my rent for living on the planet." — Alice Walker, author, womanist, activist

"When I say I'm a climate activist I mean that I am a fighter for the planet and a better future for EVERYONE!" —Vanessa Nakate, climate activist

"You can't change any society unless you take responsibility for it." — Grace Lee Boggs, activist, philosopher, feminist

"Anyone can change the world, no matter how small you are."— Amariyanna "Mari" Copeny "Little Miss Flint", activist, philanthropist and the youngest national Women's March ambassador

"When we're together, there's so much strength... How can you not be inspired by women who have been to hell and back over their children? You know, fighting, trying to find justice. How can you not be inspired and want to continue fighting?" — Connie Greyeyes, Indigenous Cree activist

CHAPTER THIRTEEN

Activism

"Saudi Arabia will never be the same again. The rain begins with a single drop."— Manal Al-Sharif, author and activist

"No pride for some of us without liberation for all of us." —Marsha P. Johnson, LGBTQIA+ liberation activist and performer

TAKING ACTION

For millennia, humanity has responded to inequity and abuses of power with movements, protests, and revolutions to spark change and advance progress. Over the course of our journey together in this book, we've talked about feminist activism in its many forms around the world.

It's fair to say that as I type, someone is plotting and organizing to make change in their school, community, country, or beyond—and thank goodness!

Throughout the tumultuous political and cultural realities that have rocked the world between 2016 and 2021, I've devoted time to reflecting on how history informs the present, and the more just future we're aiming to build. I often ask myself questions like, "What ties the uprising of working-class women marching to the House of Lords and Commons in London in 1642 to decry unjust laws, to reproductive rights activists achieving the largest demonstrations in Poland since the fall of communism, to Stacey Abrams and other Black women grassroots organizers in Georgia to advance voter rights and combat voter suppression in Georgia?" (Therefore sealing the ascension of the United States's first Black woman and South Asian woman vice president, Kamala Harris.)

Each of these movements advanced feminist values, perspectives, and made an indelible mark on history, but not all of them uniformly branded themselves as inherently feminist with a capital F, and that's okay. At its core, the heart of what feminism means to me is still defined by the late voter rights, gender justice, and civil rights activist Fannie Lou Hamer's call to action, **"Nobody's free until everybody's free."**

A too-often unsung hero, Hamer's legacy deserves as much recognition as the cis male leaders of the civil rights movement. Hamer, a former sharecropper who grew up in poverty, faced mortal threats and intimidation while battling the segregationist and sexist political establishment in Mississippi and organizing and registering disenfranchised voters. Proving detractors wrong who critiqued her lack of institutional power and formal education as a sixth-grade graduate, the former Senate candidate and cofounder of the National Women's Political Caucus, riveted audiences with her commanding presence, unapologetic speaking style, and moral clarity.

When I contemplate how Hamer's legacy relates to movements across the ages, common threads are a sense of collective consciousness, or shared ideas, beliefs, values, and knowledge within a group or society. And a commitment to collective action, where a group of folks come together to take progressive action to improve conditions, expand access, dismantle barriers to justice and freedom, or other shared goals.

That's why I'm compelled to tell you just one of my personal stories about how an indignity I experienced inspired me to take local, then national, and later global action against an injustice that is extremely close to home: street harassment. When my consciousness was raised as a result of understanding I had a shared experience that I could do something about, I worked with others to take collective action—and will continue to do so for the rest of my life. Here's my story.

FANNIE
LOU
HAMER

TAKING BACK THE STREETS

Once, a strange man yelled something vulgar in my face, and it was a breakthrough moment. Here is what happened. I learned what street harassment is when I was six. During this first time, I was walking with my then, thirty-seven-year-old mom through a construction site; we were headed home from the Al-Khozama Hotel a few blocks away from our home in Riyadh.

It was 1986, and we had been living in Saudi Arabia as American expats for several months. While we waited for our landline telephone to be installed, we used the hotel telephone every week to call relatives thousands of miles away in the Carolinas. "Habibti," he hummed in what I had learned to recognize as a Syrian accent. I didn't understand why this stranger called my mom "beloved." He didn't know her. My mother gasped, squeezed me closer, and said, "Emshi" (Go away) before hurrying her pace. As we walked quickly along the road, I heard the footsteps of the man behind us. When he reached us, he blocked our passage. And in heavily accented English, he said, "You are so beautiful, can I meet you? I need to know your name and your phone number."

My mother glared at him and replied, "Leave my baby and me alone" in broken Arabic. Disappointed, the man began to curse us. The only words I was able to translate were those that meant "Black" and "b**ch."

While my mother hurriedly pushed me into our high-rise apartment building, I asked her why she was so frightened. Naively, I wondered whether that man we encountered simply wanted to "get to know her." I didn't understand why she clenched my hand so tightly when the man had presented himself to us with what I translated as kind words.

My mother explained that the man intended to know her "in the biblical sense" and that, sadly, there were men in the world who did not know how to respect women like my father did.

Later, I heard Mom tell the story to Dad. Outraged by the fact that the man had been so boorish as to catcall a woman, let alone one walking with her daughter, she told him how scary it was to be followed. In hushed tones, Mom talked about concepts I still didn't fully understand yet, such as racism and stereotypes about American women being **hypersexualized** in the media and therefore perceived as "easy"—especially Black women and girls like us.

As you already know, my mother had been a civil rights activist in the 1960s and had endured verbal and physical abuse due to her fighting for herself and her community. Now, we were seven thousand miles from home, and she bemoaned that "walking being a woman and Black" still resulted in harassment.

Twenty years later, I had a flashback of that night, right after I was catcalled and heckled next to

Washington Square Park in Manhattan. Since I was studying at New York University, I went to read in the park regularly.

I strolled through the park, delighted to be finishing the semester, and soaked in the sunlight. A short distance from me, a blond man in his forties was standing in a suit and tie. As I passed him, he greeted me with a calm "hello." And when I raised my head, he shouted lewd comments about my body. My face twisted as he burst out laughing. He teased me by saying it even louder in a singsong voice, and then made a vulgar gesture with his fingers.

Disgusted, I watched the passersby silently observe my humiliation. I burst into tears, while the man kept saying nasty things about my body. The familiarity of his belittling gaze reminded me of having witnessed the harassment of my mother at a young age. While I was crying, I recalled past experiences: from the screams of "black and beautiful" and "brown sugar," to being forcibly touched and kissed without my consent by a delivery man, to seeing masturbation in public as a teenager in Saudi Arabia first and then in Italy as a study-abroad student. I was tired of these repeat demonstrations of degrading intimidation—and

I knew it wasn't likely to be my last experience because of the frequency of this kind of traumatic violation.

Since that day, I have been sharing my stories, denouncing harassment, and rebuffing perpetrators through my storytelling, bystander intervention, and direct-action activism and training with organizations like Hollaback!—a grassroots movement focused on ending all forms of harassment.

Harassment and sexual violence are always about abusing power and exerting control, full stop. By using verbal and physical tactics to keep us "in our place", making us "exotic," or undermining our presence with name-calling or minimizing comments, abusers foster a hostile and toxic environment.

Although the experience I shared happened on the street, the same root causes and power imbalances are reflected in our classrooms, boardrooms, transportation systems, and other public spaces due to misogyny, patriarchy, white supremacy, homophobia, ableism, sizeism, transphobia, anti-Semitism, Islamophobia, and other forms of dehumanization. From my childhood to the present, these claims of disrespect have gone to the man who felt entitled to pull on my dreadlocks on the subway because he was "curious," being called "Miss N-Word" by a white man from Oakland, and being sent unsolicited and non-consensual lewd photographs via AirDrop.

Abuse and objectification are not a joke. Due to the purveyors of this myth, it is a commonly accepted lie that unwanted sexual advances, invasive and insensitive remarks, and unsolicited touching is something we asked for, warranted due to our attire, or "just a part of life."

ENOUGH

I often think about the grim reality that 60% of women have experienced street harassment at some point in their lives and that transgender people face particularly high rates of public discrimination.

Harassment remains a pervasive cultural problem, and there is no community that is immune from it. I often hear the disturbing falsehood that Black and Brown men are more frequently guilty of harassment. My personal experience with molesters of various races and the fact-driven study of harassment maps show that street harassment crosses socioeconomic, racial, and ethnic lines.

Street harassment has been a frustrating factor in my life wherever I have lived it, from Riyadh, Saudi Arabia, to New York, New York, from Baltimore, Maryland, to Rome, Italy, and this is unacceptable.

We all deserve to have equal access to public spaces and to remain safe and free within them.

STATE OF THE STREETS

There's nothing new about sexualized violence and abuse, but the movement to stop it is gaining traction. Here's a quick snapshot of some recent movement history that led us to where we are today. Although the rise of digital video helps us capture more incidents of harassment, the toxic impact of abuse is much more common than what we see in plain sight.

The 1940s–1970s: Recy Taylor, Betty Jean Owens, and Joan Little helped spark the civil rights movement by mobilizing Black communities, giving much-needed context to how African American anti-rape activists and organizers such as Rosa Parks and Ida B. Wells inspired their communities to stand up for Black women's dignity and bodily integrity.

1960s–1976: International Take Back the Night protests rose to popularity as a way to confront violence against women and girls in Belgium and England in the 1960s. What began as demonstrations about women not feeling safe to walk home alone at night became a global movement, and a nonprofit organization that aims to end all forms of sexual violence, including street harassment.

TAKE BACK THE NIGHT

1970: Karla Jay led the Wall Street Ogle-In action where women marched on Wall Street with signs addressing street harassment. Reversing power dynamics of gender roles, women catcalled the cis men they passed on the street in hopes of raising awareness of the nature of the street harassment women experience daily.

Rosa Parks

134

1994: Deirdre Davis penned an article explaining the five common components of street harassment, including the fact that it takes place in public spaces, it happens most often between men and women, "thanking" a harasser ignites continued harassment, comments often allude to what is not visible on the target's body, and comments are often objectifying and/or demeaning even if they are masked as compliments.

2008–2012: Stop Street Harassment began as a blog and formed into a nonprofit to help people take community action against harassment and abuse.

2010: Stop Street Harassment launched International Anti-Street Harassment Week.

2010: Hollaback! was formed in 2010 to share stories of harassment and to use training and direct action to end harassment of all forms on the ground and on the internet.

2012: Brooklyn-based painter and illustrator Tatyana Fazlalizadeh launched her Stop Telling Women to Smile street art series (which later led to a book) that placed portraits of women with messages posed for street harassment offenders in public spaces.

2014: Feminista Jones launched #YouOKSis, a call to combat street harassment that called on us to ask survivors if they are okay and need help after witnessing incidents of street harassment.

2015: Peru enacts anti-street harassment laws.

2016: Quezon City, Philippines responded to its high street harassment rate with policies against catcalling.

2018: France passed a law against sexualized harassment on the streets and on public transport, fining abusive behavior. Policies in the United States vary on a state level and are highly contentious due to disputes about the limits of free speech, expression, hate speech, and the meaning of "disorderly conduct."

2018: Saudi Arabia criminalizes street harassment.

KNOWLEDGE IS POWER

Eighty percent of women have experienced street harassment.

Forty-five percent of women feel that they can't travel to public spaces alone.

Fifty percent of women feel compelled to cross the street or find alternate routes to their destinations to remain safe.

Twenty-six percent of women claim that they are in an intimate relationship to avoid harassment and protect themselves from harm.

Eighty percent of women feel the need to stay alert when walking on local streets.

Nineteen percent of women have switched jobs to escape harassment. (Research by Rebecca Lennox and Rozzet Jurdi-Hage)

Harassment and abuse are never okay, and never your fault. But the reality is BIPOC, LGBTQIA+ people, disabled people, immigrants, and other marginalized religious or other identities are disproportionately targeted. Amid a rise of authoritarianism worldwide, the tide of harassment across public spaces and institutions is resulting in hate and violence against individuals and communities.

Harassment and abuse range from personal attacks on public transportation, to racist and sexist comments at work, to targeted disruption at voter polling stations, to police brutality and vigilante violence against protesters exercising their right to free speech, among many other forms. To change the culture, policies, and norms that allow unjust systems, structures, and behaviors to persist, we must identify the problem, speak truth to power, and take action.

To learn more about how to step into your power in the face of harassment and abuse, as well as how to understand the problem, get involved in training and community outreach through organizations including **Hollaback** and **StopStreetHarassment.org.**

CALL TO ACTION

What do collective consciousness and collective action mean to you?

Jot down a life map of your experiences with harassment and abuse. When was the first time you felt unsafe?

What does safety mean to you? Have you ever been harassed on the street? At school? At work?

What role do culture and identity play into your experience of harassment?

How do power and privilege impact how and whether you encounter harassment in public and private spaces?

What steps can you take to help address and counter abuse of power in your community? How can you step up your allyship?

If any of this is triggering, know you are not alone. Help and resources are waiting for you. Contact Crisis Text Line if you need to talk to someone immediately.

"Do not think for one minute that because you are who you are, you cannot be who you imagine yourself to be." — Jedidah Isler, astrophysicist, educator, diversity in STEM advocate

"I asked questions. I wanted to know why." — Katherine Johnson, NASA research mathematician

"Some artists want to confront. Some want to invoke thought. They're all necessary and they're all valid."— Maya Lin, architect

"The core ingredients for revolutionary leadership are this: let yourself be seen, experience joy, dwell in gratitude, dream expansively and trust yourself." —Sabrina Hersi Issa, human rights technologist and investor, Be Bold Media CEO

"I like crossing the imaginary boundaries people set up between different fields—it's very refreshing."—Maryam Mirzakhani, first woman to win math's most prestigious honor, the Fields Medal

CHAPTER FOURTEEN

Innovation

"That brain of mine is something more than merely mortal; as time will show." —Ada Lovelace, computer programmer, mathematician, and writer

"If we do not share our stories and shine a light on inequities, things will not change." —Ellen Pao, author, investor, and CEO of Project Include

WHAT DOES FEMINIST INNOVATION MEAN TO YOU?

When I think of feminist innovators, I often reflect on the life of my late mother. The fiercely formidable but tenderhearted woman I called Mommy, otherwise known as Dr. Willa Alfreda-Wilson, raised in the segregated American South, went on to become the first African American to earn masters and doctoral degrees in communication disorders from the University of Illinois.

From the start, Mom's research, teaching, and clinical interests were in the areas of international and multicultural perspectives in speech-language pathology, child language developmental disabilities, and neurogenics. When I reflect on the impact her trailblazing and intersectional research, practice, and writing had on the world, I can't help but associate her interest and passion for Black feminism with her understanding and passion for health-care justice and communication equity for all.

Although she was encouraged to be a schoolteacher, like her parents, she told me that speech pathology inspired her. As a civil rights activist and educator at the time, she strove to make both communication and diverse ways of learning a human right that would be both accessible and attainable for everyone. Her approach to her work stood in direct contrast to what a conservative cis white male teacher told me once when I challenged him with a question about how colonialism impacted his view on the true origins of an invention. "Well, Jamia, despite your desire to make everything political, science is one thing that isn't." I begged to differ as I pointed out that I still hadn't had a science teacher who looked anything like me or the people of color in the classroom, which was met with silence and a smirk.

Throughout her global career, Dr. Freda, as Mom was known by her loving students and patients, was especially interested in issues impacting underserved multicultural, rural, and remote populations from South Carolina, to Saudi Arabia, to Russia, and India. By spending many evenings and weekends in the lab with her and my father, who worked alongside her as a speech scientist, I witnessed firsthand how my parents integrated their social justice values into providing dignified and thoughtful care for all patients.

In their offices, I learned about the deaf justice movement and disability advocacy by watching my mother sign intensely with her patients and their parents. During late dinners after a long day at the clinic, my parents spoke about their research and outreach to rural children, and their concerns about regional, class, race, gender, colonialism, and immigration-related barriers impacting their cherished clients.

Since my parents worked together for over forty years, I often received questions from their colleagues when I attended talks for people in their field. "Are you going into the sciences?" Before I could jump in with a remark about how I didn't share some of their strengths, including statistics, neurology, or anatomy, my mom would say, "My baby is a writer and an activist. She fights for the right to expression and communication for all people. We work to get them access. Justice and dignity are the same business, just a different approach, set of talents, and lane."

In her final days, we sat with her doctor who noted, "I wondered why you weren't in the sciences like both your parents, but now I see that your work is tied to what they do in the world. You're doing free speech;

they help people speak." At that moment, my eyes locked with Mom's as she squeezed my hand. We shared a quick warm smile, despite the painful reasons behind us being in the hospital. We marveled because this doctor, who had dedicated much of his time to working out why the kind of uterine cancer that took my mom impacts

Black women so brutally and disproportionately, knew what we often had to explain. That moment helped me understand what I'd been learning all along from my folks—science, innovation, and social justice don't have to be siloed—in fact, they shouldn't be in order to achieve accessible, just, and comprehensive care for everyone who needs it.

KEEP CALM AND TRUST YOUR INNOVATION

When I began my first executive director job in 2013, I moved to California to lead a nonprofit organization focused on creating technology to support health and wellness for youth of all genders and backgrounds. We created youth-driven tools to help BIPOC, queer folks, and immigrant youth receive age-appropriate, comprehensive, and medically accurate sex education and health-related resources. During their first annual conference, I made my debut with a speech about how **the "revolution will be youth innovated."**

At that time, I had no idea what was to come in terms of the March for Our Lives movements, the climate justice school strikes, and many other game-changing, youth-led movements, but I did see the importance of acknowledging the headwinds of a cultural tide that would soon be coming—a new fresh perspective on power, collaboration, and working together to do good across difference, including age.

Starting with a slide that said, "Keep Calm and Trust Innovation," I sought to challenge the tired notion that the so-called Selfie Generation or the Me Generation was apathetic and superficial. Instead, I argued that the next generation is the future of humanity. By examining research by the Skoll Foundation, which showed that gross domestic product (GDP) does not equal social progress, I thought about what we're missing when we judge the possibility and progress of any people but especially young people who are marginalized in their access to resources, wealth, and privilege. That's when I realized and called for the importance of moving away from seeing youth as simply a market for innovative tools, projects, and marketing campaigns, and instead as participants, leaders, and developers of the tools we need to solve for the root cause of the problems we face as humans.

It was then that I explored how to develop the mindset, values, and courage needed to create the kinds of organizations young people need to practice and advance sustainable leadership. For me, "Generation Selfie" was and still is innovating our future and taking their rightful place as leaders, visionaries, solvers, and organizers. Before I stepped off the stage, I pledged to lead with a culture of care at the heart of my approach—but also to do what I could to create conditions to equip young people with the tools they need to create impact. As a parting remark, I said,

"If you are intimidated by those who came before you, understand you too have a place right next to them."

Now, may I ask, what is the place you hope to take? What is the space you need to make? Whose support do you need to get where you need to go? And who can you organize with to break barriers standing in the way of progress and change?

WHO INSPIRES YOU TO INNOVATE?

Here are some of my favorite innovators. Each of these luminaries helped expand my thinking about what we can all do and create in the world:

Trailblazing French filmmaker, **Alice Guy-Blaché** (1873–1968) created one of the first narrative fiction films. As the first woman to direct a film, she was also one of the first filmmakers to feature an interracial cast. Her films explored race, gender, and class.

Born in 1930, **Dr. Gladys West** is an African American mathematician whose modeling work led to the invention of GPS.

In 1964, philanthropist **Reed Erickson** (1917–1992) launched

the Erickson Educational Foundation to advance transgender studies, support trans movements, and to fund events and education for trans people and their families.

Born in 1967, **Ozlem Tureci**, a self-described "Prussian Turk," German immunologist, worked with a team to develop an effective vaccine against SARS-CoV-2, know as COVID-19.

In 1981, **Patricia Bath** was the

first African American woman doctor to earn a patent for medical purposes with her invention of the Laserphaco Probe. Bath made it possible for people like me who were born with or developed cataracts to gain more sight or be fully restored.

Scientist **Gitanjali Rao**, 15, was named *Time* magazine's "Kid of the Year" for her efforts

to address contaminated water, opioid addiction, and online harassment in 2020.

LET'S TALK ABOUT POWER

We are creators of our own future. In a truly liberated and just world, my aforementioned statement would be fully achievable. This is a proclamation I say out loud because I endeavor to push for a reality that would make this a total and complete truth. Yet we live in a reality where systemic inequality and structural obstacles stand in the way of equity, accessibility, and justice for many of us who lack the power, privilege, and resources to bring this into fruition. Although we are not yet living in a world where resources are justly distributed and access to services and power are disparate at best, we can play a role in shaping a better future together. No matter what problems we want to solve or what spaces we want to innovate in, we must understand and address power imbalances in order to disrupt systems and tools that hurt instead of help.

Do you have a vision for how we need to reimagine work, art, tech, or anything else? If you plan to innovate in science, art, social movements, or any other field, naming power dynamics and making space for centering people with less access and power to speak is an important place to start. From my perspective, a huge part of what makes innovation exciting is that invention needs creativity, process, risk-taking, and an understanding of history to make progress.

Here are some questions for you to explore as you consider how to integrate feminist innovation into all aspects of your life, whether it impacts how you ask a question in class or determines what kind of project or campaign you hope to work on to make a lasting difference in your community.

Stanford's *Center for Innovation* writes, "Social innovation focuses attention on the ideas and solutions that create social value." What kinds of solutions are you looking for to create social value? Or whose social innovation ideas have inspired you? How can you get involved and help support them?

Who has done previous work to help people understand the root of this issue? How can you cite and recognize their help in getting there? Whose voices have been left out of conversations and popular knowledge about this issue? How can you raise awareness about the perspectives that were left out?

Who can you partner with to help you make progress?

GET INVOLVED

If feminist social innovation interests you, follow the work of these organizations on social media and sign up for their mailing lists:

Frida: The Young Feminist Fund

Global Fund for Women

Hollaback!

Oxfam, The Young Foundation

The Helm

Digital Undivided

Glow Up Games

The Roots Lab

CHAPTER FIFTEEN

What Does Feminism Mean to YOU?

"The only way we stop the global reactionist wave is together, in streets everywhere, demanding what is ours: our bodies, our lives, our country, the world." —Zofia Malisz, Lewica Razem political party in Poland

"I've realized that violence against women is not always connected to being in a relationship. Instead, it happens because too many men treat all women as objects, which helps them to justify inflicting abuse against us when we choose to exercise our own free will." —Megan Thee Stallion, entertainer, philanthropist, entrepreneur

"Like racism and all forms of prejudice, bigotry against transgender people is a deadly carcinogen. We are pitted against each other in order to keep us from seeing each other as allies. Genuine bonds of solidarity can be forged between people who respect each other's differences and are willing to fight their enemy together. We are the class that does the work of the world and can revolutionize it. We can win true liberation."— Leslie Feinberg, author of *Transgender Liberation: A Movement Whose Time Has Come*

WHAT DOES FEMINISM MEAN TO YOU?

Studies show that more than half of people worldwide identify as feminists, yet persistent systemic barriers to equality and the rise of authoritarianism stand in stark contrast to this reality. While many folks agree that fostering gender equality and pay equity is crucial to a more just society, research says that most are confident that gender discrimination is unlikely to end anytime soon. How does that make you feel?

Of the population that declines to take on the label, many agree with the fundamental principles of feminism that people of all genders should have racial, economic, cultural, health, environmental, and political equality. But for some, the label is too heavy to carry because of outdated myths, misconceptions, and stigmas about suppressing cis men or promoting the superiority of one specific gender expression. Others are reluctant to take on the "F word" because of movements in the past (and present) that have mostly centered those with privilege and power, while sidelining marginalized voices based on class, ability, nationality, race, sexuality, and beyond.

When I think of this disconnect, I want to talk to more people about what feminism is and what it can be. It is essential to distinguish between how feminism has been misunderstood, limited in scope, and often appropriated into something other than its ever-expanding meaning.

No one mind or one voice defines the entirety of what feminism is and can be, and that is why it is so visionary and always on time.

Over the years, I have personally discovered that my feminism evolves and grows with time and experience. I accept and celebrate that my feminist consciousness will continue to expand throughout my life, through everyday interactions, epiphanies, struggles, frustrations, and the constant pursuit of truth. What I have learned is that my feminism is enriched by deeply listening to others and broadening my insights about what and who is missing from the conversation and the top of the proverbial agenda.

In 2014, Teresa Younger took

the helm of the Ms. Foundation, one of the first and largest women's funds in the United States. Soon after she began leading the iconic institution, Teresa and her team ignited their #MyFeminismIs campaign to embark on a comprehensive, inclusive, and intersectional conversation about equality. Even though 2014 seems like worlds away from today, I often think about their broad invitation to the public to join the 42 artists, athletes, organizers, makers, dreamers, and media makers they featured by adding their definitions and beliefs about equality, an ever-growing dialogue.

The gift #MyFeminismIs gave to me was a question that I ask myself often and with intention—every time I visit the voting booth, in my relationships, at the doctor's office, in the boardroom, at the food co-op, on the subway when I witness harassment, and on and on and on and on. What does my feminism mean to me? What does intersectional feminism look and feel like, and how can I choose to embrace, embody, and advance these values at this moment?

To be sure, my singular understanding of feminism does not reflect the myriad of ways justice, equality, and liberation for all people can and will exist in today's context and into a far-reaching future. No one mind or one voice defines the entirety of what feminism is and can be, and that is why it is so visionary and always on time.

Feminism is an idea and way of living that I approach as a praxis, promise, and practice. When I feel that my perspective or community is left out of feminist conversations in the media or the public discourse, I ponder what feminism needs to be to ensure that all of the diverse voices that make us who we are, are heard, uplifted, and supported.

What seeds have been planted that have helped you grow your mind, voice, and ability to organize with others to help us all be free?

Now it is your turn.
Jot down your
mini-manifesto.

WOMAN POWER

What is
feminism?

What can feminism be

GRL

PWR

How can I grow my commitment to equality?

How can I show up in ways that bring my values to life? To school? To work? To my art?

NOTES

1. Tarana Burke founded the MeToo movement in 2006 after speaking with a thirteen-year-old girl who opened up about the sexual abuse she was experiencing at the hands of her mother's boyfriend. Burke describes it as "a movement that deals specifically with sexual violence. And it is a framework for how to do the work of ending sexual violence." It focuses on healing and survivorship that comes from building community with other survivors and speaking out. It had existed for years but gained national attention when allegations of sexual assault were brought against former Hollywood producer and convicted sex offender Harvey Weinstein, in 2017.

2. In 1991, Anita Hill made history when she testified before the US Senate Judiciary Committee about the sexual harassment she said she experienced while working with her supervisor Clarence Thomas at the Equal Employment Opportunity Commission. President George H.W. Bush had nominated Clarence Thomas to replace Thurgood Marshall on the Supreme Court, and Hill told the FBI that Thomas sexually harassed her. Thomas denied her account, and his defenders aimed to destroy her credibility, accusing her of being a liar. The open hearing was televised to millions of viewers across the country. Hill, just thirty-one and a young African American law professor, faced a panel of mostly older white men's questions about the harassment. This was a turning point for many people in the country watching who identified with what she said. At the time, Joe Biden presided over the hearing. He called and questioned witnesses and controlled the pace of cross-examination. Biden was criticized for failing to call witnesses who corroborated Hill's experience, and for the undignified way Hill was questioned. Biden recently called Hill to express "regret for what she endured." ★

3. This is due to the reality of who held the most access to platforms to publish their perspectives, stories amplifying the struggles of cis heterosexual middle and upper-class white women became the focus of how gender identity and feminism is understood. As a result, the challenges they personally experienced—related to voting, education, and marriage policies, customs and laws—became the center of the feminist conversation.

4. The Combahee River Collective was a Black feminist lesbian organization that gathered between 1974 and 1980 to address their needs as a community, to write about their identities, and to declare that collective, nonhierarchical power creates a pathway for culture and society to defy and stamp out gender, sexual, racial, and class-based domination and oppression.

5. Take the time to research where candidates of all genders stand on gender equality, racial justice, immigration, health care equity, reproductive rights, and climate justice to get a full picture. To be sure, achieving simply "fair" gender representation does not ensure equity or equality. As we've seen through several examples throughout history and the present, some women officials embrace policies that undermine progress and advancement for marginalized groups. For this reason, and more, taking an intersectional approach when looking at who to support during elections is an important consideration.

FURTHER READING

You Have the Right to Remain Fat, by Virgie Tovar

I Love Myself When I Am Laughing, by Zora Neale Hurston

Bad Feminist, by Roxane Gay

What We're Told Not to Talk About (But We're Going to Anyway): Women's Voices from East London to Ethiopia, by Nimko Ali

Hood Feminism: Notes from the Women White Feminists Forgot, by Mikki Kendall

Eloquent Rage, by Brittney Cooper

White Tears/Brown Scars, by Ruby Hamad

Women, Race & Class, by Angela Y. Davis

Sister Outsider, by Audre Lorde

Daughter of Destiny, by Benazir Bhutto

Letter to My Daughter, by Maya Angelou

In Search of Our Mother's Gardens, by Alice Walker

A Taste of Power: A Black Woman's Story, by Elaine Brown

All About Love, by bell hooks

Feminism Is for Everybody, by bell hooks

So Here I Am: Speeches by Great Women to Empower and Inspire, by Anna Russell

Everyday Sexism, by Laura Bates

The Beauvoir Sisters, by Claudine Monteil

Thick and Other Essays, by Tressie McMillan Cottom

Men Explain Things to Me, by Rebecca Solnit

Perfect Girls, Starving Daughters, by Courtney E. Martin

GLOSSARY

Absentee vote—a vote cast by a person who, because of absence from the usual voting district, illness, or similar, has been permitted to vote by mail.

American dream—the ideals of freedom, equality, and opportunity traditionally held to be available to every American. The ethos of the American Dream emerged from the Declaration of Independence which states that "all men are created equal" with the right to "life, liberty and the pursuit of happiness." The idea of the American Dream is often discussed and debated in terms of who is able to access it, who is systemically blocked from attaining it, and who is given support in attaining it.

Asexual—not involving sex or sexual feelings; nonsexual.

Authoritarian—a form of ruling that rejects diversity within a political party, favoring the use of power to control the status quo. For example, an authoritarian government might reject freedom of religion, hold a fraudulent election, or exercise power without restraint in regard to law.

Autonomy—independence or freedom from external control or influence.

Benevolent sexism—a form of sexism in which people, especially women, who conform to traditional gender roles are viewed in a positive manner.

BIPOC—an umbrella term that stands for "Black people, Indigenous peoples, and people of color." A more empowering term than "minority." Used when referring to a group rather than an individual. In the UK, BAME (Black, Asian, Minority Ethnic) is often used, while still noticing its limitations.

Bluestocking feminists—a name, now often used in a derogatory way, for an intellectual or well-read woman. The original story of the Bluestockings began in eighteenth-century Britain, when groups of women came together to discuss social and educational matters with men. They were usually wealthy and conservative, but their meetings were fairly radical for the time and place.

Capitalism—an economic system in which wealth is made and maintained by private individuals or businesses, especially as contrasted to co-operatively, government-, or state-owned means of wealth.

Choice feminism—an individualistic approach to feminism, stating the individual choices of a woman are always feminist, because she made them herself. It is problematic, as it disregards the limitations set by race, sexual orientation and identity, ability, and/or class and doesn't account for power dynamics or structures in society.

Cisgender (cis)—a person whose gender identity corresponds with that person's sex assigned at birth.

Civil rights organizers (United

States)—people involved in organizing marches, boycotts, and extensive efforts of civil disobedience, such as sit-ins, as well as voter education and voting drives. Most of these efforts were local but made a national impact in the struggle for social justice that took place mainly during the 1950s and 1960s for Black Americans to gain equal rights under the law in the United States.

Color-blind framework—an ideology that tries to dismantle racism by treating individuals as equally as possible, without regard to race, culture, or ethnicity. However, it can cause harm through not seeing people in their wholeness, rejecting cultural heritage, and ignoring negative experiences or denying disadvantages experienced because of race.

Consciousness raising—increasing awareness of social conditions that cause and maintain injustice. An approach popularized by 1960s feminists.

First-wave feminist—early feminism in the nineteenth and twentieth centuries that focused on political power, mainly voting rights for white, middle-class women. In most cases, it did not consider and fight for women of color or women of lower socioeconomic status.

Food deserts—neighborhoods where poverty, poor public transport, and a lack of big supermarkets limit access to affordable and fresh food.

Freelance economy—where companies hire workers to complete specific tasks for a one-off payment on a short-term contract, rather than a permanent position with a regular salary.

Gaslighting—a form of emotional abuse in abusive relationships. The act of manipulating a person by forcing them to question their thoughts, memories and events, which as a result, can lead to the person questioning their sanity.

Gender nonconforming—people who have a gender expression that does not conform to traditional gender norms.

Global majority—an empowering term that reflects how Black people, Indigenous peoples, and people of color represent over 80% of the world's population. This wording points out the inaccuracy of the term "minority."

Heteronormative—behavior or attitudes consistent with traditional male or female gender roles and the assumption of heterosexuality as the norm.

Homogeneity—composed of parts of the same nature or likeness, rather than of different kinds and types.

Homophobia—dislike of and or prejudice against LGBTQIA+ people.

Hypersexualize—to accentuate the sexuality of something.

Hypervigilance—a state of increased alertness. If you're in a state of hypervigilance, you're extremely sensitive to your surroundings. Hypervigilance is often triggered by trauma.

Insurgency—rising in revolt, rebellion, or resistance against authority or an establishment.

Internal conditioning—the process of training or accustoming a person to behave in a specific way or to accept a certain situation or set of norms.

Intersectional—the overlap created by social identities (like race, class, gender), which contributes to the specific type of discrimination experienced by an individual.

Jim Crow laws—laws that enforced racial segregation in the US South between 1877 and the mid-1960s. They represented the legitimization of anti-Black racism, which treated African Americans as second-class citizens in all aspects of life. Violence was instrumental and used as a method of social control.

LGBTQIA+—the common abbreviation for the lesbian, gay, bisexual, pansexual, transgender, genderqueer, queer, intersexed, agender, asexual, and ally community.

Meritocracy—where progress is conceptually based on ability and talent rather than on class, gender, or race privilege or wealth. Meritocracy is often misconstrued as being "objective and fair" because it focuses on rewarding individuals without regard for barriers to access or unearned privilege that expedited their advancement.

Microaggressions—a subtle but offensive comment or action directed at a member of a marginalized group, that is often unintentionally offensive or unconsciously reinforces a stereotype.

Misogynistic—disdain for, dislike of, and or ingrained prejudice against girls and women.

Monocular—having vision in only one eye.

Monogamous—the practice of having only one mate.

Mujerista—a term that places Latinx women and nonbinary folks at the center of a feminist movement, rather than as an "Other," but recognizes the need for liberation for all.

Nuclear family—a social unit composed of two parents and one or more children.

Oxymoron—a figure of speech that seems to contradict itself, such as "cruel kindness."

Patriarchal—(system) relating to or denoting a system of society or government controlled by men.

Polyamorous—involved in the practice of engaging in multiple romantic relationships, with the consent of all the people involved.

Reparations—money, resources, and/or materials given, usually by a government or country, as an apology or acknowledgement for a historic wrong. It could be for a country, or for an individual, for loss suffered. In this context, reparations for Black people for the enslavement of their ancestors.

Riot girl/riot grrrl—a member of a movement of young feminists associated with punk-style rock music.

Self-actualization—the realization or fulfilment of one's talents and potential.

Separate but equal—a former policy in parts of the US, where BIPOC people could be segregated if granted equal facilities to white people, e.g. for school, jobs, transportation. In practice, the facilities for BIPOC people were almost always inferior to services for white people, or simply did not exist.

Solidarity—mutual support through unity, agreement, feeling, action, empathy, or similar struggles, especially among people with shared visions, goals, and interests.

Stock portfolios—a collection of financial investments. Someone invests in them with the hope of making a profit and increasing wealth.

Suffragist—an advocate of the extension of voting rights (especially to women).

Tampon tax—the name given to the tax charged on women's sanitary products in many countries. This is unlike the tax exemption status granted to other products considered "basic necessities." (It is not a specific tax on tampons.) This tax was scrapped in the UK in 2021.

Toxic masculinity—this term is defined by strict conformity to imposing limited notions and stereotypes of what traditional gender roles should look, feel, and sound like to all people who are assigned cis, male gender at birth. It is characterized by glorifying a set of behaviors, including dominance, stoicism, status, competition, and aggression. It shows up in the form of mocking, limiting, suppressing, or punishing boys and men who express their full range of emotions, including sadness, anger, and vulnerability.

Western—Although the concept of western culture is often expressed to describe norms and values with origins in Anglo-Saxon and Western European culture, Dr. Kwame Anthony Appiah explains that "The values of liberty, tolerance, and rational inquiry are not the birthright of a single culture. In fact, the very notion of something called 'western culture' is a modern invention."

White supremacy—the hateful ideology that white people are superior to other races, born from racism and anti-Semitism. It may also refer to the systems that collectively enable white people to maintain power in social, economic, political, and moral structures.

Womanist—a Black feminist or feminist of color who opposes sexism in the Black community and racism throughout the feminist community, with the aim of uniting women of color with the feminist movement.

Jamia Wilson is a feminist activist, writer, and speaker. She joined Random House as vice president and executive editor in 2021. As the former director of the Feminist Press at the City University of New York and the former VP of programs at the Women's Media Center, Jamia has been a leading voice on women's rights issues for over a decade. Her work has appeared in numerous outlets, including the *New York Times, the Today Show, CNN,*

Photo by Aubrie Pick

Elle, BBC, Rookie, Refinery 29, Glamour, Teen Vogue, and *The Washington Post.* She is the author of *Young, Gifted, and Black,* the introduction and oral history in *Together We Rise: Behind the Scenes at the Protest Heard Around the World, Step Into Your Power: 23 Lessons on How to Live Your Best Life; Big Ideas for Young Thinkers; ABC's of AOC;* and coauthor of *Roadmap for Revolutionaries: Resistance, Advocacy, and Activism for All.*

Aurélia Durand is a French illustrator based in Paris. Her work is dedicated to representing people of color in society, and she uses bold art as a vivid demonstration. "I use vibrant colors and joyful music to spread good vibes to talk about diversity and open a conversation about why it matters to include more color in our society." She wants to create more nuanced illustrative stories by portraying women of color standing proudly

Photo by Aurélia Durand

and fiercely. Her work has been featured in advertising campaigns, galleries, and editorial magazines. Her clients include Apple, Malala Fund, Urban Decay, Evian, and the *New Yorker.* She shares her work online on different platforms, mainly Instagram, where she posts daily illustrations, live paintings, and animations. She is the illustrator of *This Book Is Anti-Racist,* and its companion journal title. Find her on Instagram: @4ur3lia.

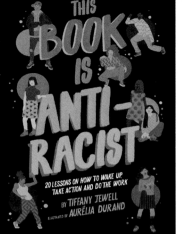

978-0-7112-4521-1

In *This Book Is Anti-Racist*, Tiffany Jewell and Aurélia Durand gave us an essential volume to understand anti-racism.

978-0-7112-6303-1

And in the companion journal, a space for your thoughts, learnings, and growth.

Brimming with creative inspiration, how-to projects, and useful information to enrich your everyday life, Quarto Knows is a favourite destination for those pursuing their interests and passions. Visit our site and dig deeper with our books into your area of interest: Quarto Creates, Quarto Cooks, Quarto Homes, Quarto Lives, Quarto Drives, Quarto Explores, Quarto Gifts, or Quarto Kids.

Inspiring | Educating | Creating | Entertaining

First Published in 2021 by Frances Lincoln Children's Books, an imprint of The Quarto Group. 100 Cummings Center, Suite 265D, Beverly, MA 01915, USA. T +1 978-282-9590 F +1 078-283-2742 **www.QuartoKnows.com**

A catalogue record for this book is available from the British Library.

ISBN 978-0-7112-5641-5

The illustrations were created digitally
Set in Cooper Black, Bitstream Cooper, Aurélia regular, and Bitterbrush

Published by Katie Cotton
Designed by Karissa Santos
Commissioned and edited by Katy Flint
Production by Dawn Cameron
Sensitivity read by Fox Fisher
Proofread by Melissa Brown Levine
Editorial Assistance from Alex Hithersay

Manufactured in Guangdong, China TT032021

9 8 7 6 5 4 3 2 1